NEW LIFE

for churches in Ireland

GOOD PRACTICE IN CONVERSION AND REUSE

Edited by Paul Harron

Sponsors:

ESME MITCHELL TRUST

First published in 2012 by Ulster Historic Churches Trust

Editor: Paul Harron
Design: g2 design
Print: W & G Baird
A catalogue record for this title is available from the British Library.

Front cover: View of Tattykeeran church and extension, Co. Fermanagh;
back cover: window details, Tattykeeran church (both photographs by Darren McLoughlin)
courtesy of Nathan Armstrong Architect

Contents

Preface   5

Introduction – The Heritage of Irish Churches   7

Conservation Principles for Converting Churches   11

Under-used and Redundant Places of Worship   15

The Role of the N.I.E.A. in Relation to the

Reuse of Ecclesiastical Buildings   18

Case Studies   Tattykeeran, Co. Fermanagh   22

Christ Church, Belfast   30

Elmwood Hall, Belfast   36

St George's Carrick-on-Shannon   42

St Mary's, Dublin   48

St George's, Dublin   54

Kilmainham Congregational, Dublin   62

Highlanes Gallery, Drogheda   68

The Mariners' Church, Dun Laoghaire   74

Triskel Christ Church, Cork   80

Carlingford Heritage Centre   86

Cork Vision Centre   92

St Mullin's, Co. Carlow   96

Teach Cheoil, West Clare   99

Converted Churches, Roscommon   102

St John's, Knockainey   104

Converting Churches into Libraries   106

Work in Progress   Portaferry Presbyterian Church   116

Duncairn Complex, Belfast   120

Carlisle Memorial Church, Belfast   124

Chapel of the Resurrection, Belfast   127

St Werburgh's, Dublin   131

Contributors   134

Bibliography   138

Acknowledgements and Credits   142

St John's, Knockainey, Co. Limerick

Preface

Ireland's ecclesiastical buildings are part of the backdrop and fabric of our lives. They are a legacy of the vision of our ancestors who built places of worship for themselves and their successors. Fortunately the majority of our churches remain in use as places of worship and are well-loved and respected in their communities. Occasionally a church or chapel is no longer required for its original purpose mainly because of demographic changes and the increased secularisation of our society. Then there is a feeling of loss and sadness which is not confined to its small congregation. However, if instead of becoming a decaying object of pity a sustainable new use can be found it may well breathe new life into the community of which it forms a part. The Trust hopes that this publication will raise awareness of the issues and stimulate further debate and discussion.

In this publication the Ulster Historic Churches Trust provides examples of best practice in the reuse of redundant and underused places of worship across the island of Ireland. There are case studies with architectural drawings and well-illustrated photographic details on completed projects as well as more modest but nevertheless important schemes, followed by a section featuring projects where work is underway but not complete. We have included schemes which range from the conversion of churches for domestic as well as cultural, commercial and community use. In one instance the future allows for combining an active ecclesiastical use alongside a broader cultural remit. All these individual studies are underpinned by an analysis of our ecclesiastical heritage, a flow chart to stimulate discussion on underused churches and an explanation of conservation principles and statutory responsibilities.

In selecting projects for inclusion we invited members of the Royal Society of Ulster Architects (R.S.U.A.) and the Royal Institute of Architects of Ireland (R.I.A.I.) to submit schemes. The schemes included are not the only examples of good practice but are a representative selection and were judged against agreed criteria.* The authors of the essays represent a diversity of public opinion – they write from an architectural, historical, clerical and lay perspective. On behalf of the Ulster Historic Churches Trust I thank them warmly for contributing their wisdom and experience to this publication.

| *Primrose Wilson*
Chairman, Ulster Historic Churches Trust

* Selection criteria – priority given to projects which: (a) Respect the original architectural design, plan form and spatial volume of the church; (b) Demonstrate a conservation-led approach to the design concept; (c) Demonstrate an understanding of the historical importance of these buildings in their settings; (d) Demonstrate an understanding of the international principles of conservation as established by ICOMOS (International Council on Monuments and Sites); (e) Address the issue of reversibility; and (f) Deal effectively and sensitively with historically important features and fittings such as memorials, decoration, stained glass and other artefacts.

Introduction

The Heritage of Irish Churches
Professor Alistair Rowan F.R.S.E.

It is a surprising fact that of all the old states of Europe, places whose history and civilization are well established, Ireland is unique for having fewer medieval churches surviving than any other country. Of the buildings of the Christian Church, founded by Patrick in the fifth century and flourishing, at least until the arrival of Henry II in 1172, virtually nothing remains intact. Monastic settlements of a quite particular, Irish character once covered the whole of the island. Groups of small single-cell, stone-built churches stood amongst wattle-and-thatch huts, protected by a circular walled enclosure; there were high crosses with an iconographical programme of scriptural scenes, and, always, a tall and tapering round tower to act as a marker and indicate the presence of the community. Round towers remain at many sites but the churches whose presence first caused them to be built survive only as minimal ruins.

When the Normans arrived they brought feudalism and a different way of doing things. Continental patterns of organization and worship meant that the forms of the Celtic church either disappeared or were modified to match the expectations of new rulers. Hierarchy was essential in the feudal age, and so, from the late 12th century, the status both of the clergy and the sacraments which they administered was enhanced by the creation of a privileged space, a sanctuary or chancel, set apart at the east end of the church. Indeed where parts of a Celtic church survive it is often the case that a chancel created by the Normans and connected by a separate arch exists as well. Every later medieval church of any size in Ireland made use of this plan. It is found in Cormac's Chapel at the Rock of Cashel, in the surviving medieval cathedrals in Armagh, Dublin, Kilkenny, Limerick and Down and it becomes the dominant pattern, with or without aisles, side chapels or crossing towers, in all the ruins of medieval churches and abbeys throughout the country.

We should note the word ruins and ask ourselves whether a country which has let most of the best of its sacred architecture fall into ruin and often disappear has served its people or posterity well? Why have we virtually none of the religious architectural heritage of England or Scotland, of France, Germany, Italy or Spain? There must be reasons for the dearth of historic churches here: the turmoil in Irish society throughout the 17th century, the viciousness of the religious wars and the practical prejudice that operated against all things old in a wet climate and devastated land. None of these can have helped, particularly where the course of the 17th century marked the end of many institutions that might otherwise have preserved our heritage. Yet faith itself was not a victim of these times. The English and Scottish planters, brought into Ireland as part of the political programmes of Queen Mary or of James I, held different views from the Gaelic lords whose families had been dispossessed: but Catholic or Church of Ireland, Presbyterian, Methodist, Quaker or Huguenot, each denomination stood firmly by its own religious principle. People still needed churches and built them once again. At first the process was halting and uneven. Old churches were patched up and, despite the Penal laws enacted by Queen Anne's parliament in

London, and the Protestant ascendancy in Dublin, even places of worship for Catholics could survive and be maintained in those parts of the country that were far from centres of power.

In the Georgian cities, a well-built church increasingly became part of the fabric of society, a place where people of consequence could meet and be seen. Fundamentally the Church of Ireland acted as an organ of the state. Here new legislation was made public; acts were read out to the congregation, and in garrison towns the attendance at church of government troops and their officers added an extra edge to the symbolic value of the building. As a consequence the new churches erected in the reigns of George II (1727-60) and George III (1760-1820) are expressive of the power of the ruling elite. Invariably they were generously planned and handsomely built in a robust sort of way and even today they make an undeniable contribution to the sense of place and quality of the environment wherever they are found. The Presbyterian, Catholic and other nonconformist congregations could not, of course, aspire to architecture of any grandeur. Soon after 1690 Presbyterian ministers achieved a degree of accord with the government, and the simple churches which they were permitted to build, either as square stone boxes or more commonly on a T-shaped vernacular plan, were soon to be used as patterns by the Catholic clergy who, with the gradual relaxation of the Penal laws, started to construct chapels from about the middle of the century. The sum of money that was available to build these Catholic churches was necessarily small: in the Georgian age they had rubble walls, floors of baked earth tiles and thatched roofs.

It was the Act of Union of 1801 which launched the 19th century as the greatest period of church building in Ireland. Soon after the Dublin parliament ceased to exist the government in Westminster embarked upon an Irish church-building programme, designed to appease the ruling classes who had lost power, by providing the funds to enable the Church of Ireland – little more than ten per cent of the population - either to expand or to rebuild its property. The money was provided through the Board of First Fruits and in about 25 years a huge number of new and often rather toy-like Gothic revival churches, with battlemented towers and gabled halls behind, had been built in every diocese in the country. From 1828, following Emancipation, the objective of every Roman Catholic priest was to build a church appropriate to the huge numbers of people who now attended mass. At first these were big plain churches, often no more than larger versions of the Board of First Fruits type or – more common in the Irish towns – ambitious Classical temples whose style reflected the Continental experience of clergy who had been trained abroad.

By the middle of the century each of the major Protestant denominations had evolved a characteristic building type: the Church of Ireland built Picturesque Gothic churches of a small to moderate size, always observing the traditional pattern of a nave for the congregation and a chancel for the clergy; Presbyterians favoured rectangular Classical halls, two-storeys high with galleries round three sides of the room, focusing on a pulpit and communion table and Methodism, which stressed the preaching of the word, made use of large open halls which might be Classical or Gothic. In the late Victorian period the Presbyterians and other nonconformists tended to adopt late Gothic Revival forms and other eclectic styles often of a fanciful decorative character. The Catholic Church, which was particularly active in this period, developed an ambitious form of elaborated Gothic design where a wide and high nave, often roofed in wood, is flanked by arcaded aisles with a high altar and side chapels at the eastern end. As emigrants to America prospered and could support church-building projects at home, the ambition of priests and their architects grew, so that some of the richest and grandest late Gothic churches in the country, complex in plan and silhouette, rich with polished marbles, mosaic and tiled floors, were achieved by the Roman Catholic church in the closing years of Queen Victoria's reign. These are truly splendid buildings that gather in their forms the aspirations and achievements of their age.

Now at the opening of the 21st century much of this inheritance of Irish religious architecture is at risk. It is not just that fewer people go to church today, though that certainly is the case. In many instances the Georgian and Victorian churches which have come down to us from the past, are in the wrong place. Every town in Ireland has witnessed the effects of suburban sprawl and it is no wonder that families are disinclined to travel into the centre of a city merely to support the life of an old building whose presence has been made irrelevant by the reduced number of people who live in city centres and whose setting has been compromised by commercial and administrative activities, and by traffic. In a similar way, rural districts have been depopulated leaving country churches, of every denomination, without sufficient people to support them on a regular basis.

What is to be done? Should these buildings simply be allowed to disappear as happened to their medieval predecessors or should we seek to find a better solution to their redundancy, one that may provide for a degree of continuity in the future? It has long been fashionable to consider urban renewal as a process starting from the premise that the past can be swept away. Yet our churches, whether annihilated by traffic in city centres, or standing neglected in the countryside – bereft both of congregations and of purpose – still stand as powerful symbols of the values and beliefs of previous generations and of the individual histories of men and women in the past. More than this, they are built of irreplaceable materials – bricks baked in Irish kilns, stone quarried and worked locally, timber formed with a skill and understanding lost to the present age, slates from Victorian stockists and ironwork from foundries that have long since gone. Such locally-procured materials are not used by architects today yet they are an essential ingredient in the mix of our historic past. Once they have disappeared, they will never be found again and the architectural environment of the whole country will be the poorer. The problem is urgent and increasingly recurrent but, as this book illustrates, it can be addressed positively, with ingenuity and in a variety of ways.

Doorway, St. Brendan's Cathedral, Clonfert, Co. Galway

Conservation Principles for Converting Churches
Primrose Wilson & Mary Hanna

Churches, chapels and meeting houses were all erected to worship God; they are the buildings which create the environment for worship, and so are special places with a spiritual ambience. Even when the congregation has departed and the church has been deconsecrated, or the last service held, it retains its spirituality. But churches also have an architectural dimension as, in many communities, they are the most important architectural statement. Converting churches to new uses is challenging but, since their loss would significantly alter townscapes and landscapes forever, keeping them is important.

Every church, whether magnificent or humble, is a special place and represents a challenge to convert as there is no pattern to follow and the range of styles and sizes is enormous. The large inner-city Georgian or Victorian church is very different from the simple meeting house in the countryside, both in form and potential reuse. Then there are the graveyards to consider, as well as ancillary buildings which need to be retained if the sense of place is not to be lost. The most successful church conversions are those where the spiritual sense of place and the architectural issues are both addressed. This may be by the retention of the green space around the church when it is converted, or by creating a quiet space where the former chancel once was.

| Significance of place

It is essential when contemplating the conversion of a historic church to a new use to understand the significance of the building, its contents and setting. Without an assessment of its significance it is not possible to come to a realistic decision on how it should be converted and what new uses are appropriate. Preparing a statement of significance involves identifying:

its ability to provide evidence about the past
its historical associations with people and events
its setting and aesthetic appeal
its value to the local community, in both spiritual and social terms

This process is best carried out if guided by a historian or architect, in consultation with the local community and the parish or diocesan congregation. At the conclusion of the discussion an agreed statement of significance should be issued.

Church converted to a restaurant

| *New uses*

It is challenging to find new uses for church buildings as their layouts do not lend themselves to modern adaptation. Without a perfect solution it is important to find the most suitable use for the individual building. When considering adapting a church, the use which requires least intervention to the fabric is usually the best. Therefore, leasing it to another religious community or organisation should always be considered first.

Any redundant historic building deteriorates if it is not maintained, and can easily become prey to vandalism. It is important that the church is secured and regular maintenance is carried out after it is closed. Sometimes, during an interregnum when new uses are being considered, a short-term or 'meanwhile' use is proposed; this should be given serious consideration as it will keep the building in use and provide 'breathing space' to consider all the possibilities.

The forms of conversion most suitable for former places of worship are those which keep it in single-purpose use so that the open interiors and long sight lines can still be enjoyed. If these new uses are ones which do not require the introduction of large quantities of new services, this helps to lessen the impact on the building. Some possibilities for reuse in this way include concert or event venues, exhibition space, heritage or community centres.

The conversion of a church to a restaurant, office, sports facility or other commercial use is likely to have a major impact on the building. As with conversion to residential use this impact, if sensitively handled, can be minimised. There is a balancing act between finding a sustainable and viable new use for a church and compromising the building. Ensuring that alterations to the exterior of the building are kept to a minimum and extensions, where necessary, are well designed and subsidiary to the main building is important. Internally, consideration should always be given to dividing the space with screens or other movable features which retain the sense of space. Subdividing the interior to create private spaces and introducing services is not straightforward, but former vestries, galleries and transepts can be used. If there is a clear focus to the east it is preferable to confine subdivision to the west end. It is worth remembering that radically altering the character of a redundant church to suit the needs

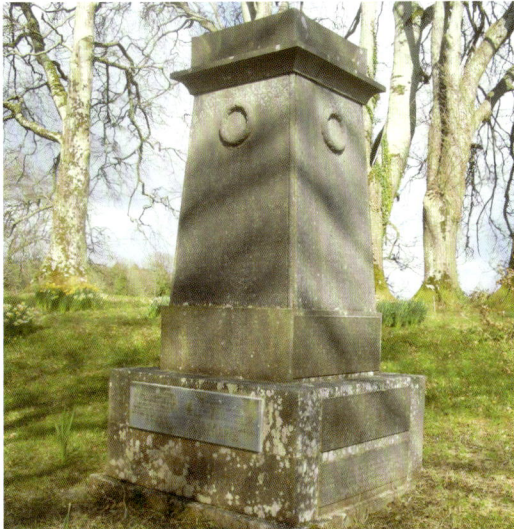
Rural graveyard

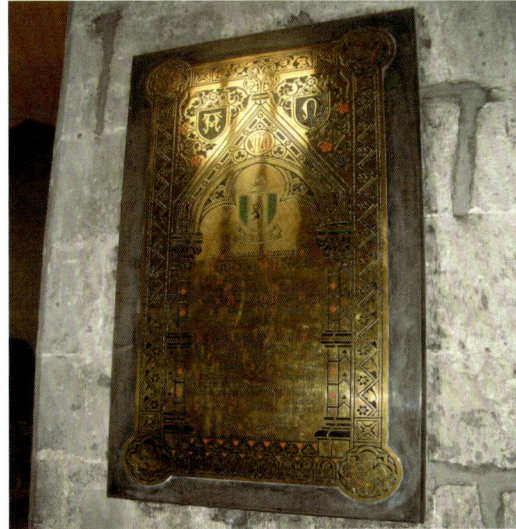
Church memorial

of a subsequent owner is a short-term approach; adapting the use to the building rather than radically altering the structure for a new use is an important principle in the conversion of all historic buildings. All interventions in a historic church should be reversible so that it can be converted to a space for other, perhaps more appropriate uses at another time.

| Memorials and graveyards

Stained glass and memorials are important elements of a church's architectural composition, and with care and sensitivity can be incorporated into and enhance the new use of the building.

Graveyards are places of great historic and aesthetic importance, as well as providing valuable green spaces in inner cities. As well as their original intended use as places for the burial of the dead, they can be tranquil public spaces for the living and valuable habitats for plants and wildlife. The presence of a graveyard may restrict the provision of new services, and a prospective owner needs to discover in advance the type of development constraints to which the site is subject.

Churches hold a special place in our collective memory, both architectural and social. While they may – for whatever reason – become redundant in active use, they live long in their surrounding community's spiritual and visual memory. While finding a new use for a deconsecrated church is both laudable and important, any prospective owner should feel a responsibility to help preserve that special visual sense of community which – often – only a church can provide.

Useful reading:
New uses for former places of worship (English Heritage) (2010)
Richard Oram, *Expressions of faith – Ulster's church heritage* (Newtownards, 2001)
Kenneth Powell, and Celia de la Hey, *Churches – a question of conversion* (SAVE) (London, 1987)
Primrose Wilson, *Maintaining our churches – a short guide* (U.H.C.T.) (Belfast, 2003)

Under-used and Redundant Places of Worship
Michael O'Boyle

In 2004, The Heritage Council of Ireland convened an expert working group to examine the issue of under-used and redundant places of worship.[1] This complex issue represents a major challenge, which will face all denominations in the first half of the 21st century. The group reviewed a range of examples of good and bad practice – including churches that had been adapted to new use; instances where a shared use had been introduced; and deconsecrated places of worship that had been mothballed or converted to new use. It considered that a good practice guide might be particularly helpful to church and parish groups in dealing with under-used church buildings. This led to the development of a flow chart as an aid in the decision-making process for such buildings.

It is important to state that the flow chart does not have a pre-determined outcome and its use does not place buildings on an irreversible path to redundancy. The emphasis is on early identification of under-use and on forward planning to secure the most appropriate outcome. The continued use of the building as a place of worship is always the preferred option. Where this is not possible, the potential to introduce complementary or shared uses should be explored. The option of securing an alternative use should only be considered as a last resort. The impact of any new use should be carefully assessed to ensure that it is compatible with the character and significance of the building.

The flow chart sets out key items of information that should be established – including the likelihood of redundancy; the architectural and historical significance of the building and its fittings; the persons and groups with whom consultation should take place throughout the process; and a range of shared uses and/or possible new uses that might be appropriate to safeguard the future of the building in the long term. The usefulness of this approach was assessed in two case studies conducted by the author in 2004.

The first study looked at a cluster of buildings (five churches and one parish hall) within a Church of Ireland parish in the Diocese of Cashel and Ossory. All of the churches were under-used to varying degrees and the closure of one or more of the buildings could be regarded as likely in the medium term. One of the churches was constructed in the 1970s and was of limited architectural or historical significance. The remaining buildings dated from the 18th and 19th centuries (possibly earlier in one case) and were all of some architectural importance. The flow chart was effective in establishing the relative significance of each of the buildings and in identifying factors that might impact on the potential to adapt the buildings to shared or new use. These factors included the location of the building, the presence of stained glass, memorials or other features of artistic significance, and the potential to introduce drainage and other modern services. The stakeholders with an interest in each of the buildings were noted and a number of particular local factors were identified. The study indicated that the flow chart provided a useful framework for the assessment of a group of buildings in declining use and in allowing for forward planning within the parish. Ultimately, this might facilitate the consolidation of activities into a smaller and more manageable group of buildings; and the adaptation of one or more of the remaining buildings to a compatible new use.

The second study comprised a review of a Church of Ireland church in Eglish, Co. Offaly, which was already redundant. The church was deconsecrated in c.1984 and was disused for the remainder of the 1980s and throughout the 1990s. The deteriorating condition of the building was a cause of concern to the local community during this time. In 2000 a non-denominational group of local people set up the Eglish Church Restoration Group Ltd., and purchased the church from the Representative Church Body. The objective of the group was to maintain the building in the short term; and to actively seek to identify an appropriate new use, which might lead to the sensitive restoration of the building and its long-term sustainable reuse.

The study was particularly useful in testing the later stages of the flow chart, which focus on the assessment of potential new uses. The complexity of the site emerged as a key issue. The church is surrounded by a large number of graves and its grounds are known to have archaeological potential. Like many rural churches, there would be difficulties in accommodating the running water and drainage provisions that would be required for some potential uses. It is suggested that owners are proactive in resolving these matters in advance of offering their church for sale. This will involve input from suitably qualified professionals. Consideration should be given to making any transfer of ownership that involves a new use conditional on the purchaser obtaining the relevant statutory consents. This would remove the risk to the building associated with a delay or a failure to obtain the necessary permissions and would ultimately benefit both vendor and purchaser.

Both of the case studies showed the flow chart to be a useful and flexible tool in facilitating the decision-making process. The example of Eglish Church highlights the importance of a programme of ongoing preventive maintenance in providing time to allow for an appropriate new use to emerge. This need not involve significant cost and in many cases would entail little more than the removal of debris from gutters and downpipes twice a year; the identification and repair of slipped slates; and periodic airing of the building.

The flow chart has potential to assist in forward planning for any church building, regardless of its level of use. There is a strong emphasis on understanding the significance of the building. The process encourages engagement with all stakeholders, whether they are members of the immediate congregation, the local community, or interested parties within wider society. Early use of the flow chart may be helpful in identifying measures to facilitate the continued or shared use of a church, which might defer the possibility of redundancy indefinitely. The ultimate objective of this process is to achieve the conservation of the building. It is hoped that the framework provided by this flow chart might help to inform and facilitate the input of all who are in a position to assist in achieving that goal.

Note:
1. The group comprised Primrose Wilson (chairperson); Ruth Delaney; Paul Arnold; Mona O'Rourke; Fr. Tomas O'Caoimh; Mary Hanna (then Architectural Officer, The Heritage Council); Ian Doyle (Archaeologist, The Heritage Council); and Michael O'Boyle.

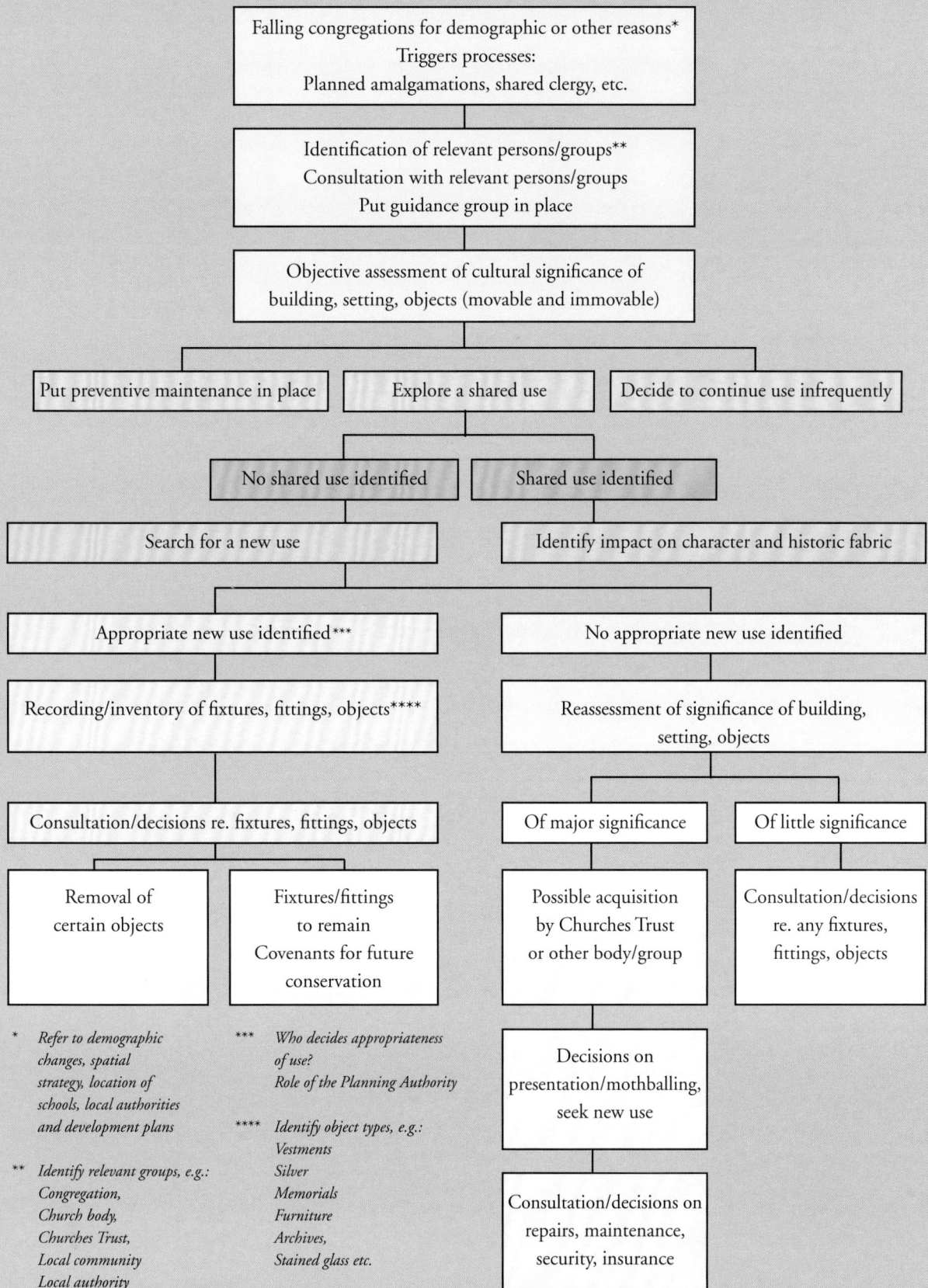

Falling congregations for demographic or other reasons*
Triggers processes:
Planned amalgamations, shared clergy, etc.

Identification of relevant persons/groups**
Consultation with relevant persons/groups
Put guidance group in place

Objective assessment of cultural significance of
building, setting, objects (movable and immovable)

Put preventive maintenance in place

Explore a shared use

Decide to continue use infrequently

No shared use identified

Shared use identified

Search for a new use

Identify impact on character and historic fabric

Appropriate new use identified***

No appropriate new use identified

Recording/inventory of fixtures, fittings, objects****

Reassessment of significance of building,
setting, objects

Consultation/decisions re. fixtures, fittings, objects

Of major significance

Of little significance

Removal of
certain objects

Fixtures/fittings
to remain
Covenants for future
conservation

Possible acquisition
by Churches Trust
or other body/group

Consultation/decisions
re. any fixtures,
fittings, objects

Decisions on
presentation/mothballing,
seek new use

Consultation/decisions on
repairs, maintenance,
security, insurance

*   Refer to demographic
    changes, spatial
    strategy, location of
    schools, local authorities
    and development plans

** Identify relevant groups, e.g.:
    Congregation,
    Church body,
    Churches Trust,
    Local community
    Local authority
    Heritage Service

*** Who decides appropriateness
    of use?
    Role of the Planning Authority

**** Identify object types, e.g.:
    Vestments
    Silver
    Memorials
    Furniture
    Archives,
    Stained glass etc.

The Role of the N.I.E.A. in Relation to the Reuse of Ecclesiastical Buildings

Historic places of worship tend to be the dominant public building type at the heart of every urban and rural community across Ulster and to a large extent all of Ireland. They generally conform to an established historical pattern and evolution which appears to be common throughout the island. Valuable repositories of the social and cultural memory of local communities, they are in many instances the only surviving example of local masonry techniques and materials – with the finest of local and imported materials used in their construction, fittings and fixtures.

Many of these churches have survived in rude health without major intervention. In fact, most began to suffer the effects of water and damp ingress when interventions were undertaken, mostly in recent years, wherein their physiology has not been properly understood and modern damp treatment techniques have been espoused – whether through the application of sealants, the removal of lime mortars and pointing and the replacement of the same with cement-rich material for renders and re-pointing of exposed stone facades. This is frequently exacerbated by the replacement of leaking cast metal rainwater goods with plastic lookalikes; the diameters of the replacements are unable to cope and distort under the pressure of increased levels of rainfall associated with climate change. The maintenance of gulleys is often overlooked and a building may sit in an impervious landscaped setting, leaving little scope for good drainage away from the building's fabric. All have resulted in increasingly damp fabric in many of our most important buildings.

Unfortunately many church bodies do not normally consult with N.I.E.A. on works to their listed historic churches. Church congregations and their consultants are aware that the current state of planning law allows alterations and removal of internal fittings within a listed church without recourse to N.I.E.A. Ecclesiastical Exemption, as it is known, means that listed buildings which are currently used as places of worship do not need listed building consent for works of alteration or removal of interior fittings. Any proposal to materially alter or extend a listed church would require planning permission in the normal way. However, once the ecclesiastical use ceases, the building is treated as a secular building. This means that planning permission and listed building consent will be required for any proposed works, including change of use and removal of fixtures and fittings.

The best way to ensure the survival and upkeep of an historic building is to keep it in active use and the best use of all is that for which it was designed. In the case of church buildings, this is particularly apt, given the complexity of volumes of space, the hierarchy of spaces and the attention to detail of the fittings and fixtures. Many ecclesiastical buildings are located in sacred grounds. This often makes the reuse of listed places of worship particularly challenging.

The preservation of façades alone and the gutting and reconstruction of interiors, is not good conservation practice. Potential owners of former church buildings are urged to contact N.I.E.A. as early as possible to discuss any proposals for reuse. A proper assessment of significance is vital to arrive at a realistic idea of what is possible for a particular building. The use of accredited conservation specialists is advised in all cases to provide advice on the repair and restoration of fabric. These specialists are not always expert in proposing interventions where they may be required and it may be worthwhile combining the services of a number of specialists.

N.I.E.A. has set out the following principles of good practice for conversion of listed places of worship:

| *Exteriors*

It is essential that the character and setting of the building is not diluted by any proposals for change of use. Existing openings should be retained and reused wherever possible. There is no potential for new openings save on minor elevations whereby additional openings for health and safety reasons may be considered. Stained glass and leaded lights to be reused in proposals for change of use.

Extensions should be modest, suitably scaled and always play a subordinate role. As in all extensions to listed buildings, the design should be carefully considered and proposals should never extend beyond principal elevations. The issue of balance of new and old must always be addressed and in some circumstances, a well designed contemporary extension, as a departure from the parent building may be a more appropriate means of addressing any imbalances.

Sensitivity to context and the use of traditional materials are not incompatible with contemporary architecture. It is important to use materials and building methods which are as high quality as those used in the existing parent building. That is the challenge to both client and architect. There may be instances where new work is designed specifically to match the original building. In such cases it must do so in all respects. Landscaping can never be used as a tool to mask bad or poor design.

The primary form of the former place of worship and retention of same is key to a successful scheme. This extends to the historic roofscape and careful consideration should be given to the retention of existing rooflines. The addition of lifts, rooflights, skylights, slate ventilators and chimney stacks of brick or stone can be visually disruptive and should only be added with in-depth and detailed consideration and discussion with Building Control and N.I.E.A.

The blocking up of doors and windows should be minimised. If unavoidable, then recessed infilling should be used on the external side, so that the outline of the door or window is still visible. Windows and doors may also be blocked from the inside, using the same principle, but keeping the door or window intact. The addition of subdivision of floors across windows is highly problematic causing visual disruption which should be avoided if possible.

It is important that markers used to identify the history and associations of the structure are not removed or masked in the proposals for change of use. Plaques, memorial tablets etc. should be retained as key elements in their original location.

All external walls should be retained with the original lime based finish or if misguided 'repairs and improvements ' in the form of cement render and waterproofing agents have been undertaken, care should be taken to remove same and replace with breathable lime render. Sand and cement pointing should be removed on exposed stone walls, particularly if strap or raised pointing has been undertaken. Deciding how and when to undertake these works is best left to a conservation architect or engineer who specialises is the repair of stone structures.

The renewal of doors and window openings should be sympathetic in design to the existing structure and be in scale with the primary building. Doors and windows and new openings should be placed so that they do not conflict with the existing harmony of openings on the primary structure.

It is critical that external features, such as boundary walling, hedging, gates and railings within the curtilage of the building be retained in proposals. Close boarded fencing, domestic paving and domestic scaled enclosures are rarely successful and should be avoided. Natural boundary features should be retained.

The construction of garages and ancillary storage accommodation should be avoided if at all possible within the curtilage of the building. If a necessity, they should be placed as inconspicuously as possible away from the building, close to boundaries, constructed with particular reference to scale, materials and detailing.

| *Interiors*

The principle of 'minimum intervention' into the primary space should be the key driver to the retention of the primary interior experience. Efforts to retain as many of the room spaces as possible without destroying their original plan form should be paramount. Listed places of worship are largely open plan with some minor ancillary rooms accessed from the main volume and this should be the guiding principle when considering suitable new uses.

The original entrance hallway should be retained, together with stairways. The creation of an additional porch or weather break should be avoided.

Stairways and galleries are an integral part of the building design and efforts should be made to retain original staircases in their original positions. The addition of separate stairs as additional means of escape may be considered in light of 'Change of Use' applications. Galleries should be retained in proposals, together with railings and detailing. Raked galleries can become attractive areas overlooking the principal spaces.

Whilst it is preferable, it is not always practicable to retain all original fittings such as pews and seating and lighting. Efforts to retain as much of the interior fittings should be made. Consideration should be given to the provision of a detailed inventory of all contents, e.g. gifts of glass, altars, marble tablets, flags and memorial plaques.

It is preferable to retain the original volume in part, if not all of the main vessel of the interior space. The insertion of a first floor can be technically challenging and visually disruptive both from the interior space and from the outside. If a gallery is present this will make it easier to locate and the gallery supports may be utilised to provide the structure for the new floor. The relationship of any new structure to the external envelope must be kept to a minimum. It is always preferable not to support intermediate floors off the external walls but to use a free-standing arrangement independent from the original building. If there is no gallery then the windows will tend to be long and usually cut across the newly inserted intermediate floor. This gives rise to the problem of hiding the floor structure from the outside and may also require additional fireproofing against spread of flame. Considerable professional skill is required to ensure that detailed consideration of all results in a pleasing internal and external handling of the matters, thus avoiding visual incoherence.

Other internal features, such as ornate plaster covings, friezes, niches and screens should be preserved and protected. Partitions etc. should be constructed in such a way as to avoid damage to these features with the potential that they can be easily removed should the structure revert back to a single volume in the future.

| *Caroline Maguire*
Historic Buildings Unit, Northern Ireland Environment Agency (N.I.E.A.)

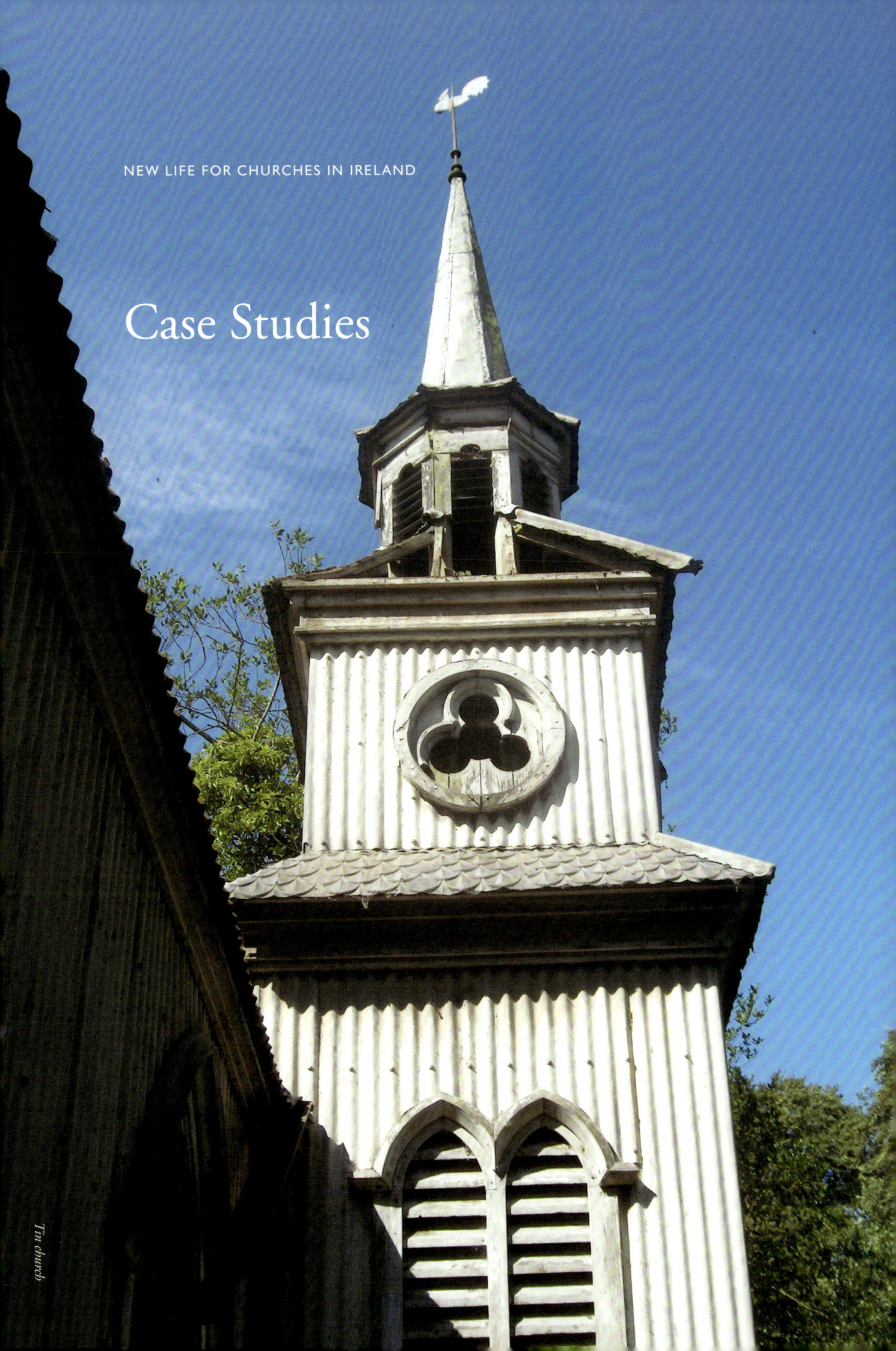

Case Studies

North East façade of church and gable wall of extension

Tattykeeran, Co. Fermanagh

Harmony in the landscape

Mindful of a lack of distinctiveness in house design in Ulster and particularly of the lack of a culturally placed architectural norm, David Brett and Alan Jones produced a challenging treatise *Toward an Architecture: Ulster in 2007* suggesting the need for Northern architects to 'build our own authenticity'.[1] Furthermore, the track record in showing care and respect for historic buildings and finding imaginative uses for redundant structures has been, at best, patchy; champion voices such as Marcus Patton, Director of Hearth, has rightly argued strongly for retaining the irreplaceable patina of age that comes with our historic built heritage, noting that 'deconsecrated churches in particular can provide excellent new accommodation for a variety of purposes'.[2] With this in mind, the treatment of the conversion of a disused country church and the design of a new adjoining wing as a contemporary home in Co. Fermanagh, by architect Nathan Armstrong, is notable. Armstrong's design of a family home for his parents is a well judged and clearly conceived piece of work. The residence respects the past while being wholly of the present, is culturally intelligent and is firmly rooted in the local landscape.

The setting is bucolic, with the deer of nearby Colebrooke Estate roaming around it. The listed church itself is simple and modest, yet charming and venerable – it dates from 1814.[3] Its attractiveness, alas, did not save it from closure in the 1980s: inoperative from 1984, it was bought by Armstrong's father, Jimmy, in 1996, in a state of considerable disrepair. Alistair Rowan described the former Church of Ireland structure as 'A pretty three-bay hall, harled, with quoins and stone surrounds to slender Gothic lancets. Bellcote and porch. Finials on the gables. A stone on the E gable is inscribed "Erected by the Rev. B. Brooke 1814". Pretty miniature gallery inside, and E window with red, white, blue and yellow glass in square panes.'[4]

Armstrong recognised that the church provided an opportunity to provide a unique dwelling, and that the single volume of the old place of worship could be a dramatic domestic space. He conceived a studio home needing four bedrooms, so his initial challenge was how to create the required accommodation. As it is not

Entrance with spiral stair to mezzanine, looking through 'link' to sleeping wing

Former church interior with mezzanine pod

Downstairs bedroom in sleeping wing with view to old church

a big church, he chose to locate the bedrooms and bathroom in an entirely new wing accessed via a wood-clad link corridor, leaving the church volume to accommodate the daily living spaces with a cantilevered oak-clad mezzanine structure providing a sleek upper studio.

Arguably the inclusion of the mezzanine is at the expense of enjoying the full airiness of the church volume and it does partially obscure the view from the entrance hall of the former east window; however, it has been restricted in size to one third of the floor-plate area, and it is ultimately a sound choice in that it is clearly demarcated as new within old and a potentially reversible component. The dining space is open to full height and still feels airy while the mezzanine opens at its far end with double doors and a glass balcony to reveal the east window and dining area below, thereby making the mezzanine studio itself more than an enclosed box. There is precedent, too – the church had originally been galleried at the west end, so the mezzanine is a nod in that direction. The architect describes the mezzanine as 'a tidy swallows' nest apparently suspended from the internal roof soffit': an appealing idea. It can be used as a multipurpose studio or an additional bedroom, and there is a bathroom located on the rear wall. This north wall is lit by newly punched discreet windows (there were, rather oddly, no original Gothic windows on this side of the church).

The kitchen and a downstairs toilet are tucked under the mezzanine, with bespoke cabinetry ensuring the minimum clutter to the living space. This cabinetry, along with the joinery in the rest of the house, has been very competently handled by a local craftsman, Draperstown-based Patrick Small, who worked on the project during its two-

Oak-clad 'link' passageway

and-half years of development. This living area, which, like the dining area, is double-height, also benefits from the three deep, tall and low bays with attractive Gothic lancets. These plain glass windows have been carefully restored, their fine window bars forming a simple, delicate tracery, allowing light to flood in. The walls have been taken right back and, like the ceiling, remade, and left a simple white. While the original coloured glass which Rowan described may have gone from the east window, a remnant of blue and yellow glass within it allows a simple pattern of colours to bounce across the walls of the living area.

The mezzanine is accessed via a bespoke spiral staircase from the entrance hall – itself accessed through a small porch which retains its original red and yellow floor tiles and a cute but rather clumsy original window (perhaps an example of a dodgy tradesman ripping the church off in the past?) – which is separated from the living area by full height glazing. In an attempt to clearly express the form of the mezzanine volume within the church shell as a new element it projects slightly past the face of the glass into the entrance hall, the entrance hall wall becoming a striking composition of glass, steel and oak. The floor from the entrance hall through the whole living space is in clean French limestone.

The sleeping wing – which is externally clad entirely in cedar – contains four double bedrooms and a downstairs bathroom. This wing is reached by a transitional 'link' where there is a distinct change of materials from hard to soft and natural – Irish oak sourced from Galway used throughout internally (with French oak for the floors). The link itself (with a simplified Gothic roof) is also finished internally in the warm oak and contains a reading niche perched within a deep bay window. From the niche, to one side can be seen – through glazed accordion doors – a serene Japanese garden beyond a foreground of finely detailed decking and visually enclosed in the background by site perimeter cedar fencing. To the other side, one can look along the landscaped grounds towards the site entrance and the Co. Fermanagh landscape. Where there were no hedges

NEW LIFE FOR CHURCHES IN IRELAND

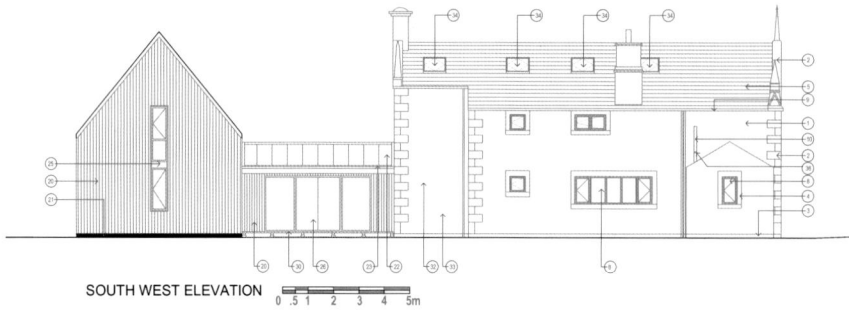

SOUTH WEST ELEVATION

0 .5 1 2 3 4 5m

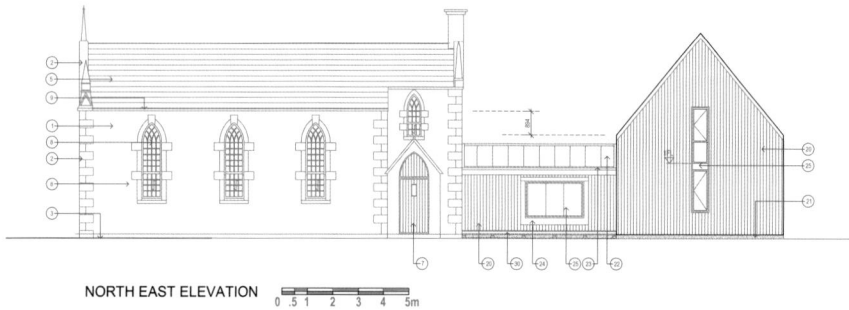

NORTH EAST ELEVATION

0 .5 1 2 3 4 5m

Elevations

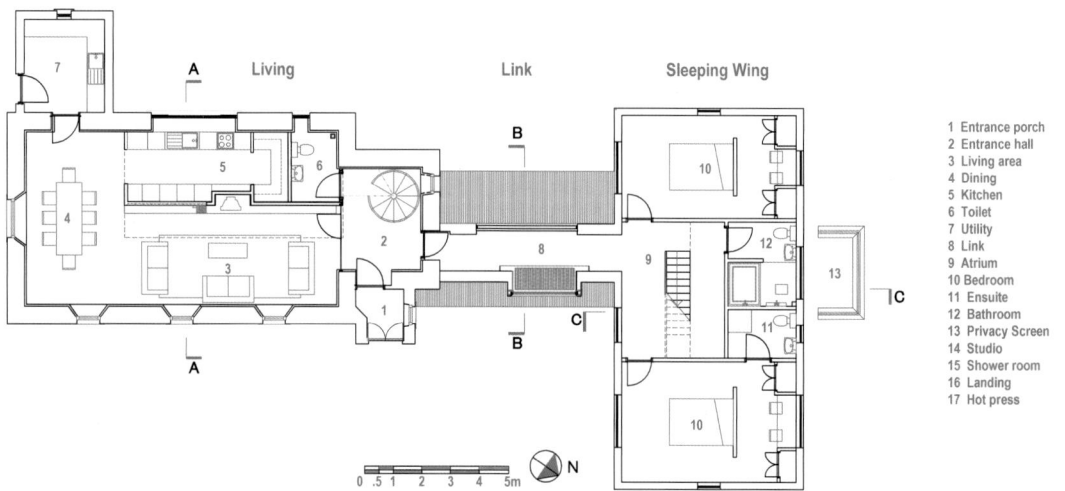

Living   Link   Sleeping Wing

1 Entrance porch
2 Entrance hall
3 Living area
4 Dining
5 Kitchen
6 Toilet
7 Utility
8 Link
9 Atrium
10 Bedroom
11 Ensuite
12 Bathroom
13 Privacy Screen
14 Studio
15 Shower room
16 Landing
17 Hot press

0 .5 1 2 3 4 5m   N

Ground Floor Plan

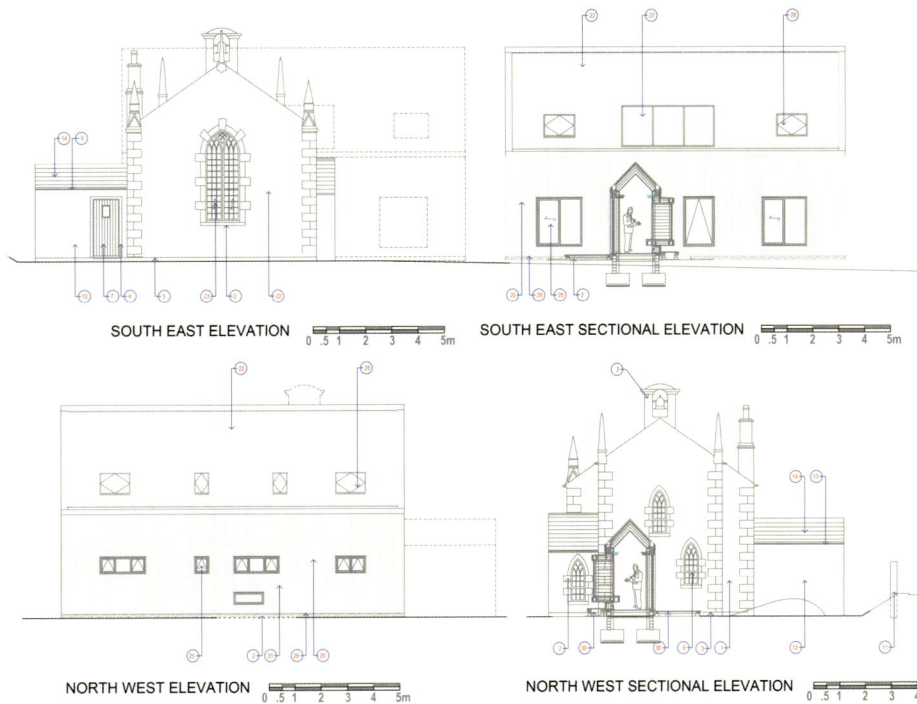

SOUTH EAST ELEVATION

SOUTH EAST SECTIONAL ELEVATION

NORTH WEST ELEVATION

NORTH WEST SECTIONAL ELEVATION

Elevations

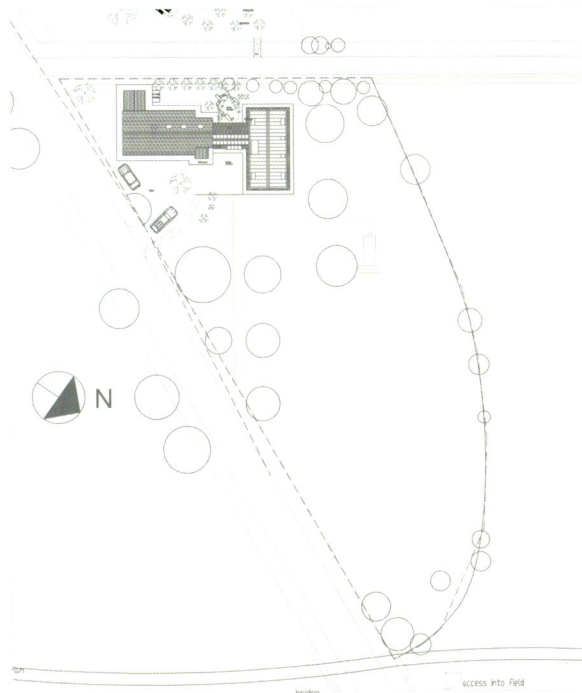

Site Plan

EXTERNAL MATERIALS KEY

1. Existing render cleaned and repaired .
2. Existing stonework cleaned and repointed.
3. Existing plaster plinth painted.
4. New plaster strapping around new windows and door.
5. Existing stone slates re-used.
6. Existing timber windows repaired where practical. Stained glass panels to be retained.
7. New hardwood doorframe and door.
8. New timber windows to church. Paint finish.
9. New half round gutter and downpipe. Cast iron.
10. New stainless steel boiler flue
11. New masonary wall rendered and painted.
12. New masonary rendered to match existing.
14. New stone slates to match existing
20. Stained vertical cedar cladding.
21. Dark grey slate plinth. Gravel edging strip to ground.
22. New light grey zinc standing seam roofing.
23. New concealed aluminium seamless gutter with internal downpipes. Zinc fascia and barge board.
24. Zinc sheet cladding and flashing.
25. Double glazed aluminium windows.Integral timber reveal board. Dark grey polyster powder coated aluminium drip flashing over profie of shallow chamfered timber sill and head.
26. New double glazed aluminium accordian timber doors.
27. New double glazed light grey polyester powder coated aluminium roof glazing frame.
28. Aluminium clad double glazed opening roof lights. Light grey powder coated.
29. Dark grey polyster powder coated aluminium drip.
30. Raised timber deck on concrete pad stones
31. Cedar privacy screen to landscaped cove.
33. GL of adjacent lane.
34. Conservation type roof lights.

View of old and new exterior from boundary fence

the boundary has been defined by cedar fencing which creates a regulated and calming design.

The sleeping wing is planned around a double storey atrium with clerestory lighting and featuring an elegant suspended oak stair which appears to lead the oak finish from the ground to the first floor. To keep the sleeping wing volume below the shoulder of the church the eaves-line is less than head height and so, to compensate, the first-floor bedrooms are double height extending right up to under the ridge of the steeply pitched roof.

Externally, this steep pitch creates a dramatic yet respectful composition perpendicular to the church: a juxtaposition of gables and rooflines which is at once both restrained and bold. It is a sensitive composition displaying a clear and harmonious relationship between the two main volumes. The architectural style of the sleeping wing is that of a contemporary barn, the barn-like form expressed by its simplicity of eaves detail, a zinc clad roof, uninterrupted vertical cedar cladding and full height slit windows to the gable. The archetype sits comfortably on this site bounded by wooded pastureland.

With repairs to stonework and re-plastering, the church building retains its original outward appearance and commands an element of authority over its new and more humbly clad neighbour, its eaves slightly higher than the other. While the proportion of the volumes is similar, the slight difference in size creates a comfortable hierarchical relationship and the materials make a clear distinction between new and old. Imagination and good judgement have come together. In addition to the Irish-sourced oak, the scheme comes with environmental credentials: a wood pellet boiler, underfloor heating and a reed bed filtration system. Robust detailing should ensure durability and the cedar's natural, untreated state will also have longevity as well as become distinguished by a silver-grey appearance over time. Tattykeeran Church has been given a new lease of life with this fresh identity as a home – it was recognised as an exceptional dwelling by coming runner-up in the 2012 BBC Northern Ireland House

| *View of the church in the landscape*

of the Year programme. Its highly contemporary addition is just the kind of accretion to a building that one would hope for: a structure which has its own firm and clear aesthetic, which is of this age and yet which interplays respectfully and imaginatively with its older neighbour but never upstages it. The 'barn' brings with it cosmopolitan influences which 'fit' – influences which speak of respecting the landscape and the setting and delighting in well considered form, just like the pretty original church with its Gothic windows and finials did, and now, thanks to this smart revisioning, still can.

| *Paul Harron*

Notes:
1. Alan Jones and David Brett, *Toward an architecture: Ulster* (Belfast, 2007)
2. Interview with Marcus Patton on BBC Radio Ulster 'Sunday Sequence', 30/11/2008
3. The church is an example of a Church of Ireland 'Board of First Fruits' church. After the 1801 Act of Union there was an unprecedented period of Anglican church building in Ireland, a boom which lasted for 30 years and covered the whole island, even its remotest parts. Hutchinson remarks, 'Amazingly, much of this building took place between 1800 and 1815, when Great Britain was engaged in a life-and-death struggle with Napoleon', Sam Hutchinson, *Towers, spires and pinnacles: A history of the cathedrals and churches of the Church of Ireland* (Bray, 2003). For further information on Board of First Fruits architecture, see also: Simon Walker, *Historic Ulster churches* (Belfast, 2000); Richard Oram, *Expressions of faith* (Newtownards, 2001); and Paul Larmour and Stephen McBride, 'The architecture of the Church of Ireland' in Raymond Gillespie and W. G. Neely (Eds), *The Laity and the Church of Ireland, 1000-2000: all sorts and conditions* (Dublin, 2002)
4. Alistair Rowan, *The buildings of Ireland: North West Ulster* (Harmonsdworth, 1979)

Background Information
Architect: Nathan Armstrong Architect

A version of this article was originally published in the R.S.U.A. journal *Perspective*, Jan/Feb 2009. It is used in revised form with permission; with thanks to the author, the R.S.U.A., Ulster Journals Ltd, Nathan Armstrong, Architect and photographer Darren McLoughlin.

Christ Church, Belfast

Handsome restoration

Christ Church, College Square North, Belfast was designed by William Farrell of Dublin in 1833 and the building belongs to the classicism of the late Georgian and the sensibility of balance and order. The handsome neo-Greek façade in sandstone, with Ionic columns in-antis, is centred upon a pedimented front door. The rear and side elevations are in brick. The lofty interior was galleried on three sides.

The space took on a different persona in 1878 when the segmental ceiling in plaster was replaced by a High Victorian renovation, the work of William Batt. Varnished pitch-pine boarding, in coffered squares, presented a permutation of patterns ranging from cruciform to diagonal layouts with central roundels in cast-iron as ventilation grilles. Batt also inserted a massive cornice and coving. The overall effect was sumptuous and sombre. A remarkable three-decker pulpit by the same architect was also added – described by Charles Brett as 'weird and impressive'.[1]

The building was an integral part of the grand vision which established College Square as the climax of the long east-west axis of Wellington Place and Chichester Street. The Royal Belfast Academical Institution (R.B.A.I.) was the centrepiece of the large open space which was partially framed by the terraces of College Square East and College Square North which included the Old Museum by Duff and Jackson as well as this building. Both were built at about the same time.

The church which had become redundant was badly damaged by fire in 1995 and apart from the structural walls, little of the original fabric survived. Some fragments were salvaged from the debris and charred rubble; these included some of the cast-iron columns to the gallery and portions of the

Front elevation

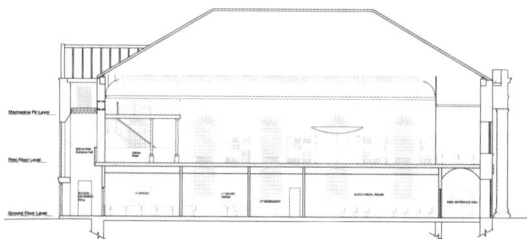

Section A-A

Section B-B

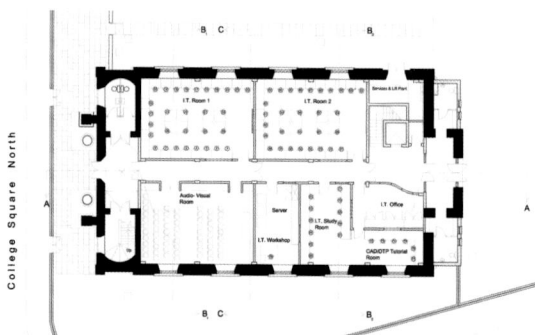

Ground Floor Plan

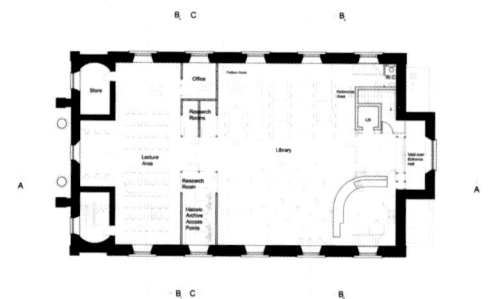

First Floor Plan

Detail of entrance lobby with tiled floor and memorial

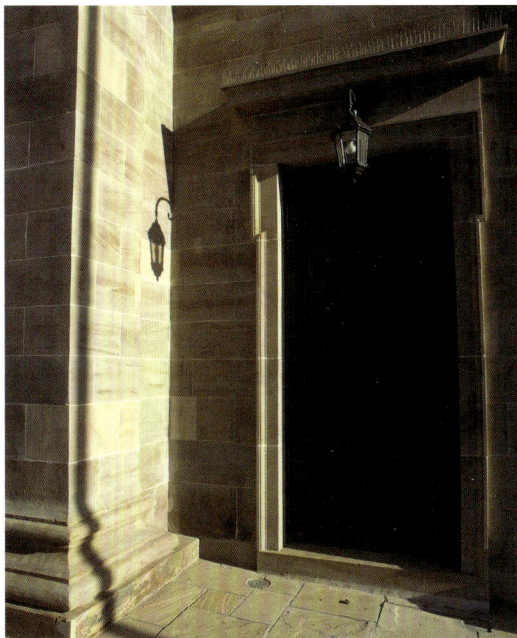

Doorway detail, front elevation

ventilators but the ceiling and cornice were lost. Fortunately the singular pulpit had been removed before the fire, as had the Robson organ, dating from the 1850s, which had been sited on the gallery above the entrance. The pulpit is now at Hillsborough Fort, Co. Down and the organ is now re-sited in the Great Hall at Queen's University, Belfast, as part of the refurbishment scheme carried out there by Consarc in 2002. Installed on the new gallery, which was part of the scheme, it is a very welcome and very appropriate addition to that interior.

R.B.A.I. had bought the building when it became redundant for use as a sports hall; however, it was found to be unsuitable for that purpose and the school built a new hall on an adjacent site. The school's earlier proposal to demolish the church was withdrawn and the building was leased to the Belfast Buildings Preservation Trust. The school became an active partner with the Trust in finding a new use for the building and in raising money for its restoration. Funding from the Heritage Lottery Fund came with the condition that the wider community should have access to the building as well as the school. The restored building should include a historic archive as a place for the study of our built heritage and the appreciation of our historic buildings. The brief also included the restoration of the historic fabric where possible and the provision of sympathetic modern interiors.

View from mezzanine to ground floor library and study desks

View from ground floor up to mezzanine balcony and replacement ceiling

Rear façade

The surviving shell was developed on two levels with access from both the school grounds and College Square North. At ground floor suites of I.T. Rooms are ranged about a central corridor running between the two entrances. The interiors belong to today and only the existing segmental windows reveal the building's antiquity. The first library and lecture rooms are separated by low-level study booths with glazed screens.

From the College Square entrance a lobby with delicate groin-vaulting leads to the restored staircase, cantilevered in stone and winding it is a vignette of Georgian elegance and economy of means. A memorial to Lady Lanyon (wife of the architect Sir Charles) who worshipped here, has been mounted in the lobby and provides an eloquent reminder of the building's architectural pedigree. School access is through the former chancel window where a new glazed entrance, Georgian in style, leads to a lift and staircase and access to the first floor.

The broad sweep of this major space is dramatized by the replacement of the boarded ceiling and cornicing. Although nothing remained of the original there was enough photographic evidence to produce what is considered a near authentic reproduction which includes the decorative ventilation grilles, cast on the evidence of the surviving fragments. Two curved mezzanine balconies at the school end overlook the space; these are carried on the surviving cast-iron columns to the galleries.

The long history of the building reflects the fluctuating tides of fashion and the changing demographics of Belfast, which made the church redundant as a place of worship. The latest phase represents a new life for the building which offers the public the chance to study the city's architectural past and it also acts as a centre of learning for the young people of R.B.A.I.

| *David Evans*

Side elevation window detail

Note:
1. C.E.B. Brett, *Buildings of Belfast* (London, 1967), p.23

This article is based and expands on one which was originally published in the R.S.U.A. journal *Perspective*, Sep/Oct 2003. It is used with permission; with thanks to the author, the R.S.U.A., Ulster Journals Ltd, Consarc and the photographer, Todd Watson, Signals.

Background Information:
Architect: Consarc Conservation

www.bbpt.org/christchurch.php

Victorian period illustration

Elmwood Presbyterian Church, University Road, Belfast

Elmwood Hall, Belfast

'Could be called Norman'

The former Elmwood Presbyterian Church was described, in the *Irish Builder*, as 'one of Ulster's best High Victorian church designs; a triumph of eclecticism, where the combination of apparently discordant elements such as a Renaissance arcade with chunky Venetian columns, mediaeval machicolations, a classical cornice and balustrade, a Moorish well canopy and a French needle spire are absorbed into a coherent but very elaborate Irish version of a Lombard Gothic church'. 'It could be called Norman' grumbled *The Builder*.

The congregation came into being as a result of the '1859 Revival' which swept across large parts of Ulster evangelical Protestant circles, with reports of over 100,000 converting through open-air preaching during the space of one year. Elmwood was the first church of any denomination to be built in what was then a developing residential area of Belfast. Belfast businessman Robert Corry gave the site for the church. John Corry, his second son and 'an amateur architect' and director of the family firm of contractors and ship owners, submitted plans which were approved at a meeting on 15th March 1859. The foundation stone was laid on 31st May 1860 and the church opened on 12th January 1862 but the tower and spire were added later, in 1872, as was the adjoining lecture hall and internal gallery. The minister's room and school rooms to the rear of the church which were also part of the original scheme by John Corry were added in 1866.

Behind the polychrome freestone façade the interior is surprisingly large, the width uninterrupted by roof supports and with a deep gallery running back over both vestibule and loggia which was reached by a winding staircase beneath the tower. Originally a substantial marble pulpit presided over this space, providing a worthy centrepiece for the elaborate stucco decoration of the windows and the coved and panelled ceiling. The church also contained some beautiful stained glass windows and a number of memorials.

Historic image

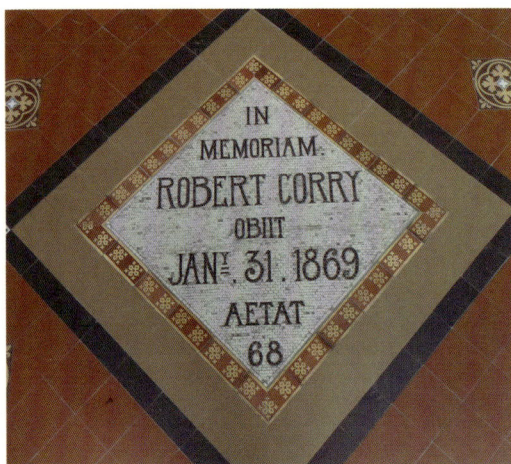

IN
MEMORIAM
ROBERT CORRY
OBIIT
JANᵺ. 31 . 1869
AETAT
68

Tiled floor to entrance

By 1966, however, Elmwood had the second smallest congregation in South Belfast. This was due to the changing character of the area. What had been a residential area was becoming more commercial due to the population moving out and buildings being taken over by business-related activities. The neighbouring university was also expanding and seeking to develop its campus facilities. By 1971 only 200 families remained and the decision was taken to close the church. The congregation, together with its minister the Reverend J. Crozier, moved temporarily to the nearby Crescent Church with the intention of relocation to a new church in Lisburn. Elmwood was purchased by Queen's University in 1971 – it was a condition of the sale to preserve the building and use it for general purposes.

During the last 19 years of its use as a church, a considerable sum had been spent on the repair and consequent redecoration of the building fabric. When acquired by Queen's University, the congregation received a purchase figure which was sufficient to build a new church and suite of halls near Lisburn. It was the intention to reuse pews, pulpit and stained glass in this new church. However, the contemporary design of the new church proved an unsatisfactory home for the original fittings so the organ and stained glass were removed to Conlig Presbyterian Church and the war memorials were repaired and are displayed in J.P. Corry's office buildings on Belfast's Springfield Road. The communion table, chair and lectern were taken to the new Elmwood Church in Lisburn.

Spire and window to gallery level

The present interior allows a flexible arrangement of seating with additional space in the gallery. The large windows along each side now have plain glass. The hall, which can seat 550, is used as a medium-sized concert hall as well as for a wide variety of events, talks and comedy shows, particularly during the annual Belfast Festival at Queen's.

From 1989 to 2009 the Elmwood Hall functioned as the rehearsal venue and administrative base for the Ulster Orchestra (the orchestra moved to new headquarters at the Ulster Hall following its restoration in 2009). David Byers, Chief Executive of the Ulster Orchestra from 2002 to 2010, loved the hall and described its strengths and drawbacks as its base:

> [Elmwood was] great, because we had the complete building to ourselves. The orchestra rehearsed in the former church, my office was the minister's room, the finance department was in the basement along with the music library, and the upstairs very large room was an open-plan office for press, marketing, development and education. We were all within shouting distance and the noise from orchestral rehearsals didn't interfere too much, if at all, with the administrative work. The box office was in the vestibule area. The balcony of the original church was seldom used, except for audiences.

> The venue was an ideal size for chamber music recitals (song recitals, string quartets and the like) and was often used for BBC recordings. It had great acoustics for small-scale music-making such as chamber music. However, there was a serious issue with the full orchestral sound. Really big orchestral works were too loud in the venue (the original carpet we inherited had been removed many years earlier and a wooden floor laid down). This made for a highly reverberant sound. Above a certain level, the sound levels, if

Interior from gallery

prolonged, would possibly cause hearing problems, hence my push to move to the Ulster Hall which has a much greater volume of space to accommodate such high levels.

Being our own home, so to speak, the layout was highly flexible, though once the orchestral risers have been positioned you don't want to move them too much. Different positions were tried to see if that would help combat the noise levels – but to no avail.

Lighting was always an issue. There were problems with sunlight blinding the players – and then having to pull the curtains. The problem was, despite having spent thousands of pounds on fitting new powerful lamps in the fabulous ceiling (a real heritage gem – like the whole building), there were always darker areas around the edges of the hall and that made reading music difficult at times … So, too, was heating that space. The electric heaters had noisy fans which couldn't be used during rehearsals and concerts. The place would cool down alarmingly quickly and become most uncomfortable for players and audiences alike.

(In conversation with the author, 2012)[1]

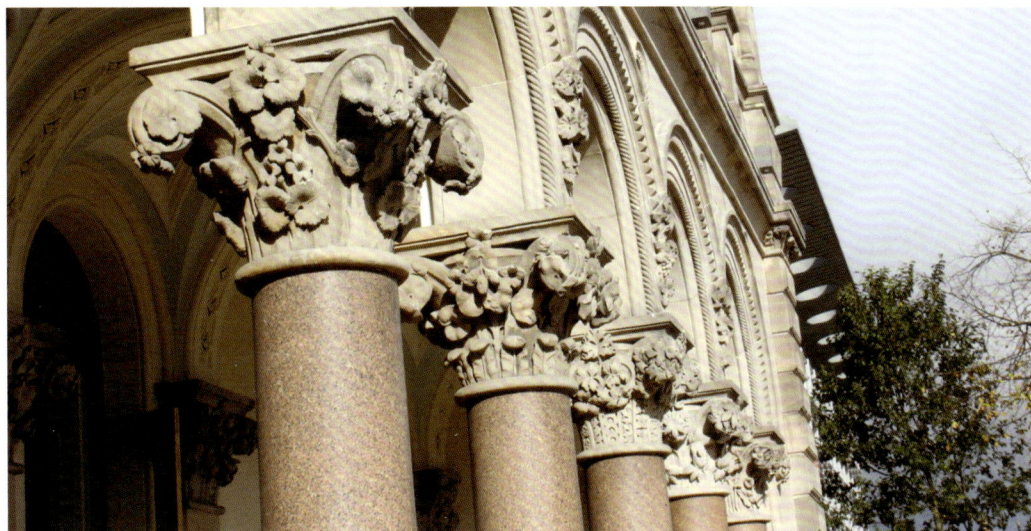

Decorated heads to columns

Queen's University has successfully maintained the building fabric, carrying out various repair schemes over the years, and continues to do so. Some stonework was restored and the golden weathercock added in 1975. The polished granite pillars had lost some of their elaborately carved sandstone capitals, but these were restored in 2000 and in 2011 the exterior stonework was steam-cleaned, defective rendering removed and new mouldings to match original detailing were added. The restoration project undertaken by Consarc Conservation was part of an overall programme to complement new buildings on the campus and to make the Elmwood Hall the university's prospective new arts centre.

The *Presbyterian Herald*, in an article of June 1971 entitled 'Elmwood: the end of an era', described the church as '…unique, as a Presbyterian place of worship. Possibly no other church in Belfast has been more photographed by students of architecture.' John Betjeman, in a Five Arts lecture at Queen's University many years ago described it as '…that splendid example of Byzantine architecture' and he would probably be delighted to see the building now thriving as part of the creation of the 'East West' link at Queen's University.

| *Jill Kerry*

Note:
1. The author is grateful for information provided by David Byers and the Revd Robert Lockhart; further useful reading on Elmwood Hall can also be found in *Perspective*, Nov/Dec 2012; the Queen's University Belfast website and in the U.A.H.S. publication, A. J. Rowan; C.E.B. Brett; Hugh Dixon and David Evans, *Historic buildings, groups of buildings, areas of architectural importance in the vicinity of the Queen's University of Belfast* (Belfast, 1980, revised edn.)

Background Information
Conservation architects: Consarc Conservation

View of exterior

St George's, Carrick-on-Shannon

Living tradition, serving its community

St George's Church was built in 1827 on a site where two previous Church of Ireland churches had stood. It is sited on the highest point of the hill overlooking the town of Carrick-on-Shannon and its elegant tall steeple, together with the tower of St Mary's Catholic Church, creates a distinctive profile to the townscape.

The church was built to the designs of the architect Joseph Welland. Most of the funding for its construction came from the Board of First Fruits which was established in 1711 to contribute to the buildings and improvement of Church of Ireland churches and rectories. The church is a fairly typical 'First Fruits' church comprising an entrance space contained in the base of a tower, with a single nave leading to a chancel, off which are two transepts. The chancel, where the communion table is located, acts as the focal point of the church.

In 1992, the schoolhouse and rectory were sold and this enabled repairs to be carried out to the bell tower. Unfortunately, there were insufficient funds to undertake the necessary works to the roof which had left the church not safe to use. Consideration was given to a proposal to sell the hall in order to repair the roof with the funds. A proposal was also made to keep the hall and use it for services and abandon the church. Thankfully this was not agreed to by the Select Vestry.

Two senior members of the Select Vestry, George Patterson and Arthur Laird, approached John Bredin about a possible application for a 'Leader Programme' running in the area.[1] It was realised that in order to finance the necessary repairs it would be advisable to link with a community organisation as this provided more funding opportunities. Lengthy discussions were held to consider various concepts and to debate what church members wished to include as part of the overall strategy.

View from East end

In 1999, a special meeting was held to discuss a feasibility study which proposed the church becoming the historical centre in the town. It was felt that the church was an appropriate venue for a centre linking all aspects of the history of Carrick-on-Shannon and the whole church congregation unanimously agreed to proceed with a 99-year leasing agreement to Carrick-on-Shannon Heritage Group. A condition of the lease was that the church would be open to the public during the week but would be available for worship on Sunday mornings and that three seats on the Board of the Heritage Group would be offered to members of St George's Select Vestry. It was felt that this was a unique opportunity for the town and it was also agreed that the sale of the church hall would be the church's contribution to the scheme and could be used to attract the various grants necessary to allow the project to be carried out.

In June 2001 the architect, Mary O'Carroll, was asked to prepare a Conservation Report for the church – a Protected Structure – which would be submitted to the Heritage Council as part of a grant application. Structurally, it appeared that the church was sound apart from the problems associated with the roof and some water damage around the windows. However, the report concluded that there was a serious amount of work required to bring the church into a reasonable state of repair and safety and to restore its historical appearance. Work was required to the roof structure and slating; stonework repairs were needed to mouldings and details; and both the exterior and interior needed plaster repairs. Damp was also a serious issue. A ramped access to the building was necessary together with appropriate lighting and power systems, a controlled heating scheme, fire and smoke detectors and suitable sanitary facilities.[2]

View towards the chancel

A partnership was formed between the Kiltoghert Group of Churches and the Carrick-on-Shannon Heritage Group and District Historical Society. The project identified St George's as an 'orientation centre' and part of an historic trail which would depict the history of the town and its surroundings, including a well-preserved section of the Old Workhouse. This provided an exclusive and unparalleled tourist attraction for the whole county. The bonus of a unique Telford pipe organ created a further opportunity for musical recitals.

Restoration works commenced on the buildings in 2003 under the direction of O'Carroll Associates, Architects and Conservation Consultants. The roof was the main focus of the work, particularly the large multiple King Post truss at the crossing of the nave and transepts. Following advice from the Heritage Council, the entire structure was lifted off the building by crane, placed on the church forecourt, repaired and then returned to its original position, all in a two day period. The steeple was re-pointed and the whole roof re-slated.

A new purpose-built Visitor Centre was erected on land to the west of the church and it allowed the necessary visitor facilities to be accommodated without interfering with the plan form of the original church. The original entrance door to the church was accessed via paired steps set on the diagonal, 900mm above ground level. A new ramp was designed allowing access to the church through an altered window opening on the west side of the tower.

The graveyard to the north and east of the church is maintained by members of the church and community and provides a welcome green oasis as well as offering additional historical interest to visitors.

The works provided the opportunity to introduce new environmentally friendly heating. Four 180m vertical holes were bored to bring geo-thermal energy under-floor heating pipes into the church and into the new

St George memorial

The Telford organ

Visitor Centre via a heat pump in the tower. This system uses a quarter of the electrical energy normally required and provides an ambient temperature of around 22°C.

In addition to these works, an electric mechanism was installed in the church clock and it was given a new face. The stained glass windows were removed, repaired and re-installed with storm glazing and the organ in its Gothic case was repaired and restored. The interior was subtly decorated with lines of text written by local authors and poets transcribed in beautiful calligraphy on to the walls above the wainscoting. Event Ltd designed a new historical banner display which can be raised or lowered in accordance with need, and which can screen the front section of the church, leaving it free for worship.

St George's Heritage & Visitor Centre was officially launched in early 2008 and includes audio/visual functions in the centre adjacent to the church. The restored church now houses a well researched and exciting historical display of artefacts and interpretive material depicting the twin traditions of Co. Leitrim from ancient Gaelic roots through Plantation times up to the county's contribution and sacrifice in the First World War. It provides a venue for concerts, exhibitions, lectures and public meetings whilst continuing to act as a place of worship. St George's Church is now fully prepared both for church services and the exhibition which contributes to the sense of wellbeing in the town and continues to serve its community locally and nationally as well as providing an exemplar to others with a dwindling congregation who wonder what to do.

| *Jill Kerry*

New entrance with ramp

Entrance door and steps

Church and Visitor Centre from graveyard

Visitor Centre

Notes:
1. Leader – Liaisons entre actions de développement de l'économie rurale – was established by the European Commission in 1991. It was designed to aid the development of sustainable rural communities following the reforms of the Common Agricultural Policy. The initiative became available in Ireland in 1992.
2. Information provided to the author from O'Carroll Associates, Architects; John Bredin, Chairman of Carrick-on-Shannon Heritage Group Ltd; and the Carrick-on-Shannon Heritage Group website: www.carrickheritage.com

Background Information
Architect: O'Carroll Associates, Architects and Conservation Consultants

Interior with view to organ case and gallery

St Mary's, Dublin

'The Church'

Enjoying your gin and tonic in what used to be the chancel of the deconsecrated church of St Mary's, Dublin, beneath an east window inscribed 'I was glad when they said unto me let us go into the house of the Lord', raises some of the questions to which this book is devoted. Are some new uses for redundant churches (libraries, heritage centres) preferable to others (bars, restaurants)? To what extent does reversibility justify interventions? And, most important of all, what lessons can be learnt from a successful conversion – such as St Mary's – which can be applied elsewhere?

Two of the fundamental, and not easily separable, elements in our experience of architecture are, on the one hand the formal and the abstract and on the other the associational: we can see both at work in our response to Le Corbusier's chapel at Ronchamp where architectural richness derives from the purely formal but also from the associated ideas of pilgrimage, miracle and the numinous.

So too in St Mary's where the splendid external frame of the east window, the rich internal carving and the great galleried space provide formal pleasures, while meaning (of some kind) derives too from the building having accommodated for centuries the worship of God and the administration of the sacraments.

So it has to be admitted that there are uneasy incongruities in the juxtaposition of gin bottles and carefully conserved scriptural texts. And the arguments of those who say that a church should not be converted into a pub are weighty. Also weighty, of course, is the argument that without the conversion, the building would not survive. The two arguments are irreconcilable. So let us turn straight away to consider the ways in which the conversion was effected.

Historic view of interior

Historic view, looking to chancel and East window

Historic view, looking to West door and organ case

The building is successful in its city setting. To Mary Street, a new glazed staircase tower articulates the corner with Jervis Street. The building forms a handsome north side to Wolfe Tone Square, recently regenerated by Dublin City Council. On street and square external seating is confined behind railings. And although tables and umbrellas are not very 'churchy', they and their customers enliven that part of town. Above them, the external fabric of the original building is rigorously devoid of neon or advertising. Such self-denying discretion is characteristic of the whole conversion.

At first sight it might appear that there is little that is discreet about the centrally placed bar running much of the length of the nave. But, unlike some recent church conversions, it reinforces the principal axis of the church. This sympathy can illustrate an answer to my earlier question 'to what extent does reversibility justify interventions?'

The nature and value of reversible work is that it is non-destructive: no material, fabric or detail is unnecessarily lost or destroyed. But some interventions, no matter how reversible, can destroy an original space for as long as they stand. With its axial position, its lack of crowning canopy or superstructure, and its discreet detail, furnishing and lighting, the bar in St Mary's leaves wholly apprehensible the 18th-century vaulted volume to which it defers.

Staircase leading to gallery dining area

On walls and ceiling, colours thanks to the researches of Richard Ireland are based on the originals. The floor is wood (happily not carpeted). The mural tablets survive without competition from more recent 'art'. And its withdrawn nature acknowledges, at least to some degree, that the original east end was a distinct and quieter space.

In the side galleries there is a restaurant and, of course, the great organ case. Its important 18th-century carving was repaired by Chaim Factor; the carving in the chancel was repaired by Dick Reid of York.

Talk of conserved carving, and repaired organ case, and retained wall monuments and inscriptions brings us to the matter of box pews. These had vanished before the recent conversion was undertaken, and it was this greatly regretted loss that made the task of the client and architects possible: box pews limit the use of converted churches, if not to meeting places of other denominations, then to auditoria.

But in St Mary's, notwithstanding compromises of bar, of extra staircase to south gallery, and of food lift from basement kitchen to north gallery, the volume of the original 18th-century nave can be appreciated, with its original and 19th-century detailing repaired, conserved and intact. Important to this is the choice of the north-east corner of the nave for entrance. Sensibly placed to accommodate pedestrians in the busy Henry and Mary Streets, it invites an unconventional point of entry to a church, from which the original meaning of the space can develop gradually.

The success of all this is due largely to the generosity of the brief which allowed for extensive excavation beneath the nave and neighbouring street in order to provide services, lavatories, kitchens and extra entertainment space. This made possible the minimal compromises of the significant spaces of nave, aisles, galleries and chancel.

Working bar and restaurant following restoration

The brief was generous, too, in allowing time for solutions to problems to evolve gradually. From the start the client was ambitious that the full significance of the building be respected: hence the employment of conservation specialists such as Richard Ireland (paint) and Dick Reid of York (wood carving). Hence the extensive excavations, and hence the discretion which was guided by the client's vision of how best the space be used.

For pub this is, but it's a particular kind of pub (and restaurant and club) with a particular kind of customer. The architectural treatment and finishing of the nave do not, for instance, suggest this as the ideal setting for a hen or stag night. And equipment for large-screen (and possibly rowdy) television viewing is – when not in use – difficult to spot. And five or six years into its present use, under new management and with its architects and original client now out of the picture, the early vision is substantially intact.

This is fortunate because, however successful a conversion might be initially, buildings have long lives. There never can be much protection against the insensitivities arising from changing requirements. The after-life of a converted building is as hazardous as the initial conversion work.

And the lessons to be learnt from St Mary's? Success depended on many things: an ambitious and visionary client; architects who were appreciative, sensitive and discreet; time to let solutions emerge. And to this must be added a large budget. But many a large budget has failed to result in good work. Many a large budget has not been a good substitute for wise judgement.

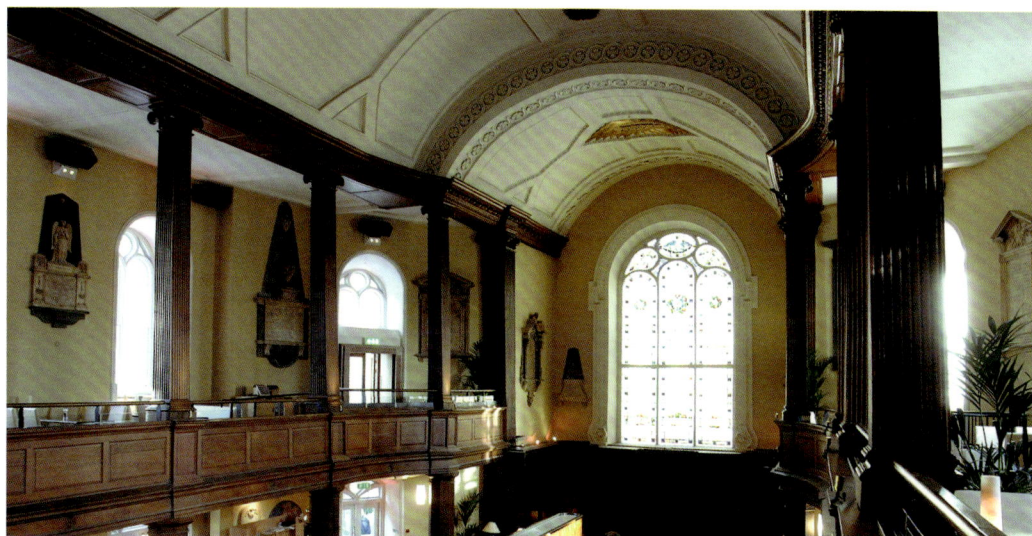

View from the gallery to the East window

So with that gin and tonic in hand, be grateful for the survival of so many of the formal and abstract values of St Mary's Church of Ireland church and reconcile yourself to the church as pub by reassuring yourself that the Ten Commandments in front of which you're sitting have as much relevance in a pub as elsewhere.

| *Edward McParland*

Background Information

St Mary's Church of Ireland church was built between 1699 and 1704. The design is probably that of Sir William Robinson, with Thomas Burgh probably overseeing completion of the works. It ceased use as a Church of Ireland church in 1981, was used by the Greek Orthodox Church until 1986 and was sold in 1986. Phase one of the conservation works began in 1998; the second phase commenced in November 2001 and the project was completed in 2003.

Conservation Architects: Shaffrey Associates Architects

www.thechurch.ie

St George's, Church of Ireland, Hardwicke Place, Dublin 1

St George's, Dublin

Integrity and attention to detail

St George's church, Hardwicke Place, Dublin was designed by Francis Johnston. He was educated at the Royal School Armagh and was for a short period architect for the Archbishop of Armagh. He moved to Dublin in 1784 and was appointed as architect for the Bank of Ireland in 1803. The Board of Works in Dublin appointed him as its architect in 1805 and Johnston was involved in the design of several important landmark projects of his era such as the Chapel Royal and the General Post Office.

In 1801, Johnston won a competition to design a new church for the Church of Ireland in Hardwicke Place. St George's was built to accommodate 'that great eighteenth century fashionable expansion in North Dublin.'[1] He was granted a generous budget with which to build a church suitable for its elite parishioners. While the Commissioners' churches which were being built in London at this time were limited to £20,000,[2] St George's cost nearly £90,000 when completed. Johnston espoused one of the major parameters which governed the ecclesiastical designs of his day, to build a church which would accommodate the greatest number of persons within the compass of an ordinary voice. In doing so, he pushed the engineering capabilities of that time slightly beyond their limits creating an impressive interior with no internal supports. In 1836 as a result of the splay in the exterior walls, Robert Mallet, a civil engineer designed cast iron trusses to counteract the thrust.[3]

The church, which has strong references to James Gibbs's St Martin-in-the-Fields, was consecrated in November 1814 and is considered to be one of Johnston's finest designs. In the 1980s stone began spalling from the tower and for safety, it was enclosed in scaffolding. One of Dublin's landmark steeples was to remain shrouded from view for over twenty years until the completion of the recent renovations as the cost of repairs was beyond financial reach of the parish. Due to the falling Church of Ireland population in inner city Dublin, it was decided that St George's should close and the final Divine Service took place on 29 April 1990.

South west facing elevation

Section B-B

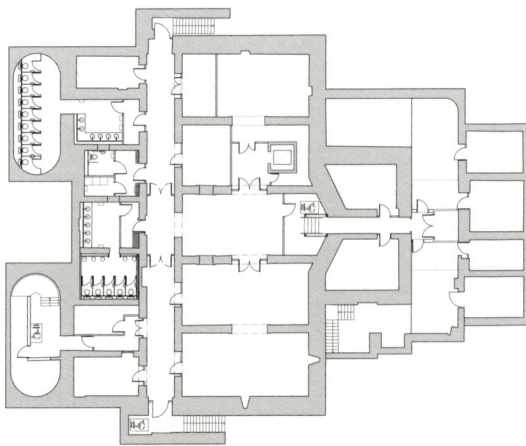

Basement plan

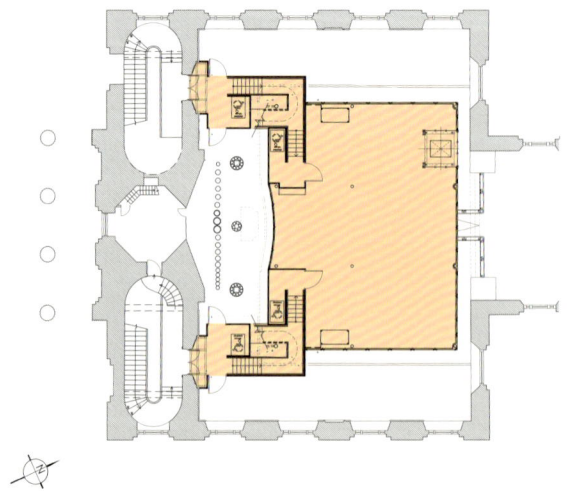

Overall second floor plan

ΔΟΞΑ ΕΝ ΥΨΙΣΤΟΙΣ ΘΕΩ

New meets old: office intervention

East stairwell

Initially the church was used as a theatre and then was transformed into a nightclub. One taxi driver who took me on a journey to St George's informed me that it had been a rather racy venue. This was not the building's first association with alcohol as the extensive cellars had once been utilised as a bonded warehouse.[4] The subsequent occupants had shown little regard for the church's interior fittings and fixtures and many of the original features had either been damaged or vandalised. New openings were unsympathetically punched into the stonework and the walls painted in a blood red and black colour scheme.

When the night club closed, the derelict building was purchased in 2004 for approximately €1.4 million by a developer, Eugene O'Connor, who wanted to restore the building and create desirable office accommodation. The restoration portion of the project was carried out by James O'Connor, whose work in Dublin includes the Academy Cinema in Pearse Street; 9 Merchant's Quay, for Dublin City Council (formerly known as Dublin Corporation) in association with Dublin Civic Trust and the James Joyce Cultural Centre at 35 North Great George's Street.

The restoration was carried out in four phases. Phase 1 included major work to the stonework of the spire which had been damaged by the breakdown of the cast iron cramps which were an integral part of its structure. The original cramps were replaced with stainless steel bands. Years of abrasion from natural elements and pollution had removed all the facial features of the exterior carvings and they were reconstructed with repair mortar. Repairs to make the roof watertight included the restoration of stones which were discoloured due to the breakdown of the lead

Upper mezzanine level

rainwater pipe-work. Extensive restoration was carried out on the external stonework of the main body of the church and portico in Phase 2 as well as the repairs to the beautiful stained glass windows which were completed by a specialist glazing sub-contractor. Every single stone on the external facades was measured, numbered and recorded on hand produced drawings before they were treated and replaced.

Alongside James O'Connor, Joseph Doyle Architects was commissioned by the developer to design a suite of offices and the two architects worked together simultaneously on Phases 3 and 4. Phase 3 consisted of the repair and restoration of the interior and the erection of two free standing floors in the main body of the church while Phase 4 – completed in 2010 – involved a full repair of the wrought iron railings, granite plinth and external paving. To fully appreciate the costs involved in such a renovation, it should be noted the repair work of Phase 4 alone cost in excess of €600,000, with the overall costs of the project exceeding €10 million. In today's financial climate it should also be remembered that much of the available grants have all but disappeared. The developer was very grateful to receive a total of €75,000 from Dublin City Council, but this was less than 1% of the total costs.

Doyle's approach to his design brief was to create a sympathetic intervention that would fund the conservation works and could be reversed allowing for the potential for the building to be brought back at a future date to Johnston's original design. It is a strange sensation to enter the main volume of the nave and experience the office suite but Doyle's innovative use of glass and steel has created a design which does not compete with or overpower Johnston's magnificent interior. The new sits neatly inside the old and both show a quiet respect for each other. Doyle's structure allows access to viewing points the original parishioners would have enjoyed experiencing. The visitor is enabled to appreciate the plasterwork close up and the view from the second floor down to the vestibule is breathtaking. Doyle has managed to create a work environment which maximises the available space without any feeling of claustrophobia. He has successfully

Staircase and mezzanine; memorials and stained glass still in situ

hidden away the services which helps to maintain the clean lines of his design and there are no jarring intrusions to compete with the building's finely restored interior. It will be a superb place in which to work for its future tenants.

The highest quality of restoration work enables a building to be viewed as it was originally without taking away the architectural narrative of the input of succeeding generations and James O'Connor's work on St George's is to be praised for its integrity and attention to detail. Joseph Doyle is to be commended for his bold approach in solving this reuse of the interior volume. His hope that the modern 'Meccano set' could be removed with minimum impact has been achieved in a sympathetic fashion.

The decision to close and sell a church building which can no longer be utilised or afforded by a dwindling number of parishioners is often a very complex and painful process. There is the added worry as to what the building will be used for in its new existence. One Presbyterian church known to me in Antrim was sold and is now occupied by a carpet showroom and tattoo parlour, something which causes consternation to members its former congregation.[5] The parishioners of St George's must be rejoicing that Eugene O'Connor has undertaken this magnificent renovation and restoration without sparing any expense. It is to be hoped that he will secure a suitable tenant in the very near future.

| *Stephen McBride*

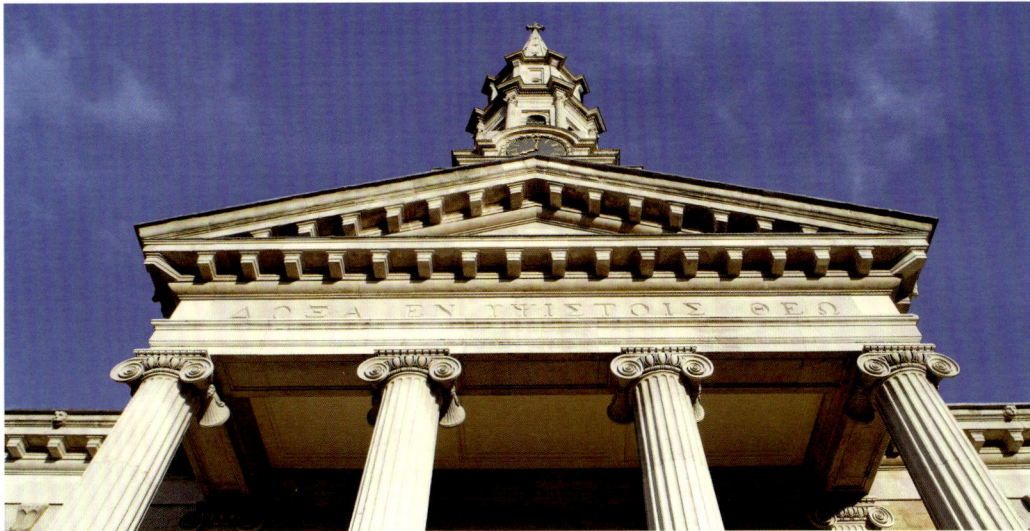

Detail of grand pedimented entrance portico

Notes:

1. R .J. Kerr, *The Parish and Church of St George, Dublin* (Dublin, 1962), p.1

2. M. H. Port, *Six hundred new churches: a study of the Church Building Commission 1818-1856 and its building activities* (London, 1961), p.61

3. Christine Casey, *The buildings of Ireland: Dublin* (New Haven and London, 2005), p.122

4. E. Cullinan, *The Irish Times,* 'Landmark Dublin church converted to offices', 25 March 2009

5. High Street Presbyterian church, Antrim of 1852 – the earliest known ecclesiastical commission by Robert Young, founder of Young & Mackenzie Architects.

Background Information

Architect: James A. O'Connor and Associates (Phases 1-2) and James A. O'Connor and Associates with Joseph Doyle Architects (Phases 3-4)

Congregational Church, Inchicore Road, Kilmainham, Dublin 8

Kilmainham Congregational, Dublin

Loaves and fishes

Set back from the Inchicore Road in Kilmainham, the former Congregational church, now elegantly converted into a three-bedroom dwelling, is a little gem of a building. Although of relatively modest architectural pretension in itself, it forms an important part of the built fabric of Kilmainham, one of the richest areas in the country for monuments to Ireland's military, charitable and religious histories. The Manor of Kilmainham was given to the Knights Hospitaller by Strongbow in about 1174, even prior to that it had been the location of an important Viking burial site, seemingly even prior to the foundation of Dublin. The Inchicore Road is dramatically punctuated at its eastern end by the monumental gates to the Royal Hospital – now the Irish Museum of Modern Art – while located just a few hundred yards from the Congregational Church are sites sacred to the collective memories of our different traditions, Kilmainham Gaol, and the National War Memorial Gardens, designed by Sir Edwin Lutyens. While all these attract visitors, Kilmainham is generally a quiet residential area, increasingly populated by young professionals with a smattering of artists; Inchichore to its west still suffers its share of urban blight.

Evangelical in spirit, and arising out of the non-conformist tradition of the 17th century, the church's beliefs are predicated on the autonomous independence of each congregation. No doubt this explains the absence of a distinctive architectural typology associated with the Congregationalists, whose buildings in Britain, Ireland and North America follow a wide variety of styles. The Kilmainham church (also known as the Salem Chapel) was built in, or about, 1814; its architect is not known, though its founder is recorded as Obadiah Williams.

The Salem Chapel was closely connected with the expanding industrialization of the area, and specifically with the nearby Hibernian Woollen Mills established in 1812 by William and Thomas Williams (sometimes spelt Willans). Samuel Lewis, writing in 1837, noted that the mills 'afford[ed] employment to nearly 500 persons, for whose residence the proprietors have erected suitable dwellings, and also a place of worship of the Independent denomination'.[1] The construction of the church was then an early

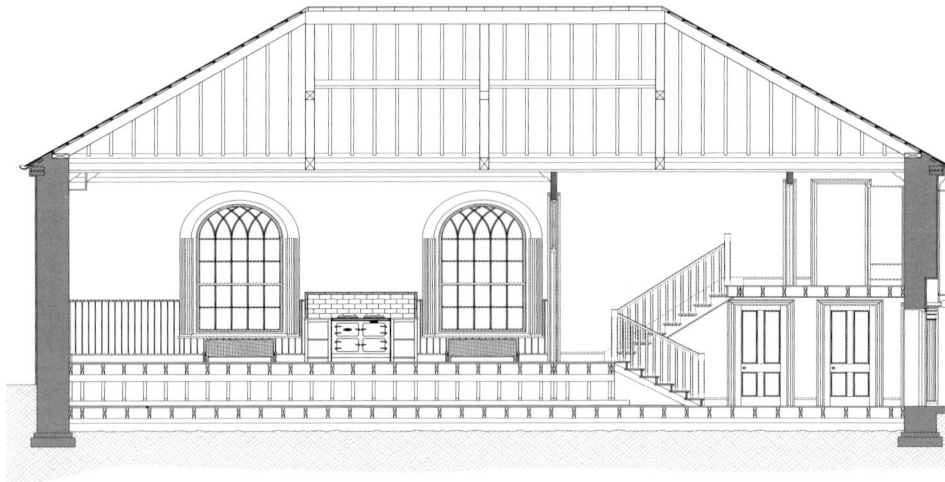

Section

example of enlightened mercantile paternalism, though the implication that the religious needs of the mills could best be met by a Congregational chapel clearly indicates its workforce was not drawn from the majority population. It is unclear whether this was from a discriminatory impulse or because of specific skills and attributes that it was felt certain religious groupings possessed – or lacked; the two motivations were of course inextricably linked.

From its inception the chapel also enjoyed close connections with Kilmainham's military establishments. A meeting held in the church in 1820 by the Hibernian Auxiliary Missionary Society gives a vivid picture of evangelical fervour: The church

> …was almost filled, at an early hour, with soldiers, the 42d Reg. and the Scots Greys being at Kilmainham barracks; several of the officers and as many of the privates as could be accommodated, attended; and it was interesting to see several of those brave veterans, who had jeoparded [sic] their lives in the fields of Waterloo, melting with tender compassion, while they heard described the degraded and perilous circumstances of the heathen world.[2]

The Congregationalists have never comprised a particularly large proportion of the reformed tradition in Ireland. In 1829 there were 28 independent congregations, compared, for example, with 372 in Wales.[3] By the millennium, the Kilmainham congregation had dwindled dramatically and a new use for the building was sought. An approach at once imaginative and sensitive was called for to retain the original fabric of the building (which is a Protected Structure) but at the same time to give it new life and purpose.

Before any alterations were made, the church was photographed and several images deposited in the Irish Architectural Archive illustrate its appearance in the final days of its almost two centuries of religious use. Acknowledging the rich archaeology of the area, test-trenching was undertaken in August 2008 and a report commissioned from Antoine Giacometti to ascertain if the nearby Viking burial ground extended as far as

Historic view of interior with pews

Main doorway looking through to tiled hall

the site and, if so, assess the risk of damage by any planned building work. However, the only remains unearthed were connected with the building of the church in the 19th century.

The residential nature of the Inchicore Road and the scale of the building itself invited its adaptation for domestic use, though less appropriate schemes were also mooted including proposals for office accommodation and for splitting the space into multiple apartments. With the building having changed hands, at least once, and having remained vacant for several years, its new owners, David and Monica Higgins and their family commissioned the conservation architectural firm John J. O'Connell Ltd to come up with plans.

A key decision was quickly made – on which rests the success of the whole project – to raise the floor level by 97cms so that the magnificent arched windows were at a height appropriate to a space configured for living rather than worship. A platform was inserted and, in effect, an 'undercroft' created where the original floor of the church is carefully preserved. The main living room, flooded with light from its twin aspects is now approached via a short flight of stairs while bedrooms are accessed from a further flight. The Georgian Gothic windows – the building's most notable feature – were painstakingly restored with a grant from Dublin City Council.

The enormous living space has been given a distinctly domestic feel through the introduction of new wainscoting and shutters which, together with the centrally placed stove, firmly anchor the room. While remarkably little has been done – apart from the raised platform – to alter the space, it no longer has the sense of being an ecclesiastical interior, unlike several other churches converted for residential use. The lack of extraneous ornament, such as stained glass, that is a hallmark of the dissenting tradition makes Congregationalist buildings particularly adaptable for domestic living – the spare lines of the building coinciding with a fashionably minimalist, 'loft-apartment', aesthetic.

Main open-plan living space

Three years of residential occupancy have clearly demonstrated the success of the adaptation from the point of view of livability. The only minor issue in terms of snagging seems be one of soundproofing between bedrooms. However, the church is of particular interest in the context of this survey in that the adaptability of the building's space, under John O'Connell's plans, has also allowed another successful – and quite unexpected – use. For a period of several months, the Higgins sisters, led by middle sibling, the Ballymaloe-trained chef, Lilly, organized a regular 'pop-up' dining club, part of the underground dining movement, called, appropriately enough, Loaves and Fishes. A not-for-profit scheme, it involved the girls cooking dinner for 30 strangers once a month, with each guest making a contribution towards costs. The main room of the house with its double frontage converted wonderfully into a 'restaurant' for the night but the familial and communal motivation behind the venture is given added resonance by the former use of the building. Where once Waterloo veterans prayed earnestly, young Dublin diners now relished good food and the companionship of strangers.

Lilly articulates the club's role in 'creating a community' in difficult economic times with a focus on co-operation and group endeavour exemplified by communal dining – by the shared breaking of bread. If the club's title is playfully witty and light-hearted, the sacramental aspect of dining fellowship seems, nevertheless, to be lurking subconsciously in Lilly's description of the supper parties as 'just like the grown up version of our Holy Communion Parties except without the fighting Grand Aunts'.[4] This is not to suggest though that the conversion of the heathen loomed large in the conversation of Loaves and Fishes diners!

The success of the conversion can be quantified on several levels. Firstly, respect has been shown to the exterior and the surrounding space. From the street little has changed, though the exterior has been rendered with a traditional lime mortar. A sign still advertises 'Kilmainham, Congregational Church'.

Staircase and doorway detail

'Loaves and Fishes' dining at the house

Although the land to the north of the church has changed hands it has not been built on and the quietude of the space is retained, uninterrupted by inappropriate extension. It is still a place of tranquillity and reflection and continues to remind us of a small part of the story of confessional identify in Dublin. From an architectural point of view the building still sits happily within its streetscape. Most importantly, all the alterations to the building are reversible and honestly identified for what they are.

That the building was converted as the recession was biting and that no effort or expense was spared in its thoughtful restoration is a tribute to the vision of owner and architect alike. The sympathetic nature of the adaptation was recognized when the building was shortlisted for both the Irish Georgian Society's Architectural Conservation Award and the Irish Architecture Awards in 2011.

| *William Laffan*

Notes:
1. Samuel Lewis, *Topographical Dictionary of Ireland* (London, 1837) vol. 2, p.170; see also Deirdre Conroy, *Conservation Report, Kilmainhaim Congregational Church, Inchicore Road, Dublin 8* (Archive Consultants, Jan. 2004)
2. *Evangelical Magazine and Missionary Chronicle*, Vol. 28 (London, 1820) p.443
3. *The Congregational Magazine* for the Year 1829, New Series no. 5 (London 1829) p.736
4. http://www.blogger.com/ profile/03805354926925972312, accessed 24 May 2012.

Background information:
Architect: John J. O'Connell Architects Ltd

Franciscan Church, Laurence Street, Drogheda, Co. Louth

Highlanes Gallery, Drogheda

From Franciscan foundation to cultural treasury

The Franciscan Order has been a presence in Drogheda for over 750 years. While the former Franciscan church which is now the Highlanes Gallery – described by Casey and Rowan as 'Late Georgian Tudoresque Gothic' [1] – dates back to 1829, in fact this winsome T-planned limestone structure designed by J. Butterly sits on the ancient site of a Franciscan friary founded in 1240. Thanks to its 13th-century origins as well as the charms of the present 19th-century building itself, it forms an architecturally important part of Drogheda's rich built heritage – a stone's throw from St Laurence's Gate and nestled above Bachelors Lane, bounded on one side by a steep flight of stone steps (the 'high lanes') echoing the town's medieval streetscape, and on the other by solid Georgian townhouses.

The history of the Franciscans in Drogheda is not without its complications – what else would one expect in Ireland?[2] – but despite thriving in the 19th century, the latter part of the 20th century witnessed marked decline and the Order decided to close the church and an adjoining residence in 2000. During the following two years meetings were held with representatives of the community with a view to deciding on an appropriate future use for the buildings. Drogheda is fortunate in possessing a municipal art collection assembled between 1946 and 1981 by an enthusiastic Municipal Art Gallery and Museum Committee, founded by Bea Orpen HRHA and her husband C.E.F. (Terry) Trench.[3] The Franciscans decided to gift the building to the people of the town as a venue to house this fine collection and provide a contemporary art gallery space. This transformation from church to art gallery was completed in 2006, the design undertaken by Drogheda-based McKevitt Architects.

The property had been maintained in good repair but presented certain challenges in being converted to its new use as a gallery along with the necessary ancillary accommodation – a café, educational spaces, offices, storage and sub-lettable space (to help sustain the gallery financially). The church also has the unusual feature of entrances at ground and at gallery level, the main street access from Laurence Street being on to the deep rear church gallery 4.5m above the main nave floor, the ground-floor access to that nave originally

Ground floor exhibition space

off the Highlanes steps. There were galleries in each arm of the T-plan and the architects had to overcome the problem of fragmented access while providing a substantial exhibition gallery floor at the Laurence Street level.

Moreover, the desire was to create a contemporary art space which retained the significant features of the existing building including a three-bay Tudor Gothic reredos with large mouldings and colonnettes rising to pinnacles; the back gallery and its staircase; and richly coloured 19th-century stained glass windows featuring rarely depicted saints.

The architects' solution was to overlay the existing church galleries with a floating floor of sufficient area to serve as a large gallery space at Laurence Street level (conceivably, the new insertions could be removed and the building returned to its original form). The interior when viewed from the front of the reredos explains the building and shows all the original church gallery fronts tucked under the new layer of floor. This upper floating floor works well as a bright and airy space to view the gallery's permanent collection. It also enables the visitor to appreciate the stained glass windows in a fresh way – they now appear almost as jewel-like light boxes. A suspended plenum ceiling below that of the original church plaster ceiling distributes services and lighting to the upper gallery.

The floor of the original church provided a lower gallery space which is articulated by the existing cluster shafts that support the deep back gallery, now over-layered by the new gallery floor. This lower gallery space is normally subdivided with movable walls which provide flexibility for gallery exhibitions.

The existing reredos which can be seen from both gallery floors becomes an integrated sculpture in the space – indeed, many artists have responded actively to and used the backdrop when exhibiting in the gallery: artists such as Thomas Brezing,[4] Diana Copperwhite [5] and Gereon Krebber.[6] Contemporary elements are harmonious with the traditional, coexisting happily, and the original fabric of the former church has been substantially retained throughout. The energetic Director of the gallery Aoife Ruane states: 'Instead of a simple white cube, the visitor enters a historical yet completely modernised space, with the original altar as a superimposing, grand backdrop.' [7]

Former altar and reredos used as exhibition space

The Development Committee had also purchased an adjoining residential building located on Laurence Street east of the church. This building together with the site of an already demolished sacristy directly to the rear provided a site which could accommodate the services – a lift, toilets, kitchen stores and plant – along with a cafe and craft shop at street level. By interconnecting these spaces, the gallery spaces can be entered via the shop and café.

The main public entrances to the gallery are either through the shop-front entrance on Laurence Street or through the 19th-century church gates and across a bridge-like ramp rising from street level to the level of the new gallery floor of the church. Cleverly, a virtue has been made of the small forecourt space between the gates and the church building, with a sympathetic contemporary sail-like structure providing shelter from the elements for visitors who might want to sit outside or have a coffee in the open air.

In all, this conversion from Franciscan church to a substantial and appealing art gallery has been highly successful both architecturally – where the transformation has been creatively and lightly handled – and from the point of view of providing an arts space which curators want to and can use for contemporary arts purposes. The gallery enjoys a strong collaborative partnership with the F. E. McWilliam Gallery & Studio at Banbridge and regularly share exhibitions. The inaugural exhibition on the life and work of F. E. McWilliam toured to Highlanes Gallery, and the year following an exhibition that had its source in the Drogheda Municipal Art Collection at Highlanes Gallery, Nano Reid and Gerard Dillon, toured to the F. E. McWilliam Gallery & Studio.[8]

Where the opportunity and funding exists to put a redundant church to a new cultural or artistic purpose then it can be one of the most successful outcomes for such a building. The 'specialness' and civic presence of the structure can be maintained for the community and within the landscape/townscape, its architectural features can be seen as advantages rather than impediments – and arguably even become appreciated more closely –

| Rear of ground floor with original window and back stair detailing

| View from altar steps across ground floor and up to floating upper gallery

and the internal volumes often lend themselves to places for display. There are challenges to overcome regarding access requirements, provision of accompanying facilities and indeed financial viability over the long term, but when opportunity, vision and commitment come together the result is especially harmonious. The Highlanes Gallery is an exemplar project in this respect, returning a cherished ecclesiastical building to the community for appreciation of the arts, giving it a future over the long term and renewing public enjoyment in it.

| *Paul Harron*

Upper gallery with original stained glass window

Entrance to gallery and shop from Laurence Street houses

Notes:

1. Alistair Rowan and Christine Casey, *The buildings of Ireland: North Leinster (*Harmondsworth, 1993), pp.240-241

2. For a good history of the Order in Drogheda, see: Pat Conlin OFM, 'The Franciscans in Drogheda', an information sheet produced by the Highlanes Gallery www.highlanes.ie

3. *Highlanes Gallery: Irish art from Nathaniel Hone to Nano Reid: the Drogheda Municipal Art Collection in context* (exhibition catalogue) (Drogheda, 2006). The catalogue contains an illuminating introduction and essay by Denise Ferran.

4. *Thomas Brezing: the art of failure isn't hard to master* (exhibition catalogue) (Drogheda, 2011)

5. *Diana Copperwhite* (exhibition catalogue), (Drogheda, 2007)

6. *Gereon Krebber: here today gone tomorrow* (exhibition catalogue) (Drogheda, 2011)

7. *Thomas Brezing: the art of failure isn't hard to master,* p.10

8. See *Nano Reid and Gerard Dillon* (exhibition catalogue). The exhibition (November 2009-January 2010) was curated by Riann Coulter.

Background Information
Architect: McKevitt Architects

www.highlanes.ie

The Mariners' Church, Dun Laoghaire

The National Maritime Museum of Ireland

From the sea, the skyline of Dun Laoghaire is attractively punctuated by two Gothic spires, the belfries of the Mariners' Church (Church of Ireland) and St Michael's Church (Roman Catholic). Both were creations of the 19th-century seaport-town and both have had a chequered history. The largely remodelled late Victorian St Michael's was tragically burnt down in an accidental fire in 1965 while 'The Mariners' as it is locally known, closed for worship in the early 1970s, there being a declining Protestant population and too many Anglican churches in the neighbourhood.

The Mariners' Church, now the home of the National Maritime Museum, was erected in 1836 to the designs of Joseph Welland for the benefit of the many sailors who were based in the then new Kingstown harbour, on board British naval vessels. All naval crew were obliged to attend Divine Service, and Mary Hamilton writing in the early 1900s describes Welsh and Cornish fishing crews along with the local congregation, crowding the church, which, with its spacious galleries, could accommodate up to 1,000 worshippers.[1]

An old print discovered by historian Daniel Gillman shows the original building as a very plain structure with only nave and transepts, and its first Chaplain, the Revd R.S. Brooke, described it as 'large and gaunt, lofty and ugly, a satire on taste, a libel on all ecclesiastical rule, mocking at proportion and symmetry, but spacious and convenient'.[2] It was originally intended that the tall church should have double galleries, but in the event only one level was constructed.

Between 1862 and 1884 various improvements were carried out by Joseph Welland which left the church in its present form, complete with a chancel raised some 6 ft above the body of the church and so accommodating a vestry room beneath; an organ loft and new entrances onto Haigh Terrace (to the west). The fine tall spire is thought to be to the designs of architect Raffles Brown.[3]

All of this work was carried out to a very high standard and was finished externally in cut granite. This meant that the centre of the Victorian town with its public open space and neighbouring Marine Hotel gardens were bounded by a landmark building of high quality. Sadly, this whole setting has been diminished over recent years by the addition of Dun Laoghaire shopping centre's multi-storey car park and poor quality apartment blocks on the Pavilion site.

Interior fitted out as museum

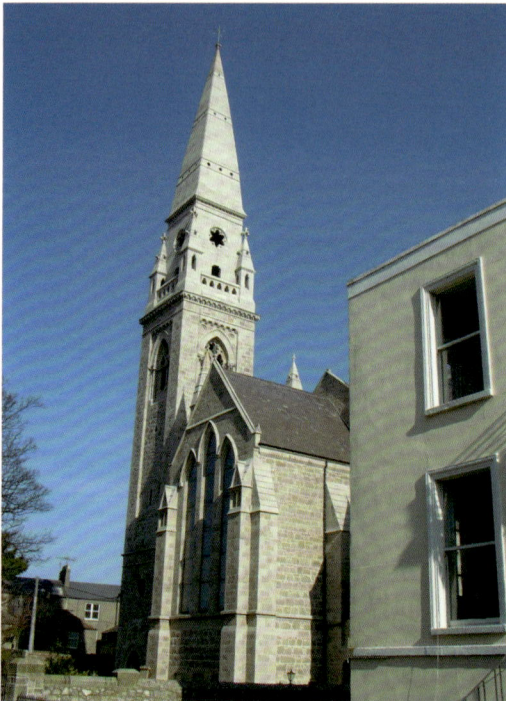

View of exterior in streetscape context

The earlier church structure was approached originally from Adelaide Street (to the east), and following the erection in the 1840s of an elaborate Gothic style residence and school abutting the east gable, the church was subsequently entered by means of a Tudor-Gothic door and a long passageway through the school.

After the closure of the church in the 1970s the school building and residence were sold separately, while the church itself was leased from the Representative Church Body of the Church of Ireland (R.C.B.) to the Maritime Institute of Ireland as its headquarters and museum, for a peppercorn rent.

The Mariners' Church was henceforward accessible only from Haigh Terrace through doorways to the North and East chancels which were intended as entrances for the clergy and for access to the galleries.

A substantial programme of refurbishment was carried out prior to the museum opening in 1974, including the removal of the pews from the galleries and main body of the church. All of the pews were made of pitch pine, had brass-numbered, Gothic panelled doors and special umbrella stands with drip trays.

New staircases were fitted to provide access to the display areas in the galleries and tiered floors were levelled. Two interesting pews, known as 'the prisoners' dock' were left in situ, and are said to have been used by the Royal Navy when prisoners under its charge were present.

During further substantial refurbishment work on the building undertaken from 2005 to 2011, conservation architect James Slattery discovered that the early structure had been externally rendered, but this was removed during the 1860s when more grandiose cut stone additions were made, in order

Stained glass window detail

to create a more unified and visually pleasing stone 'effect'. It is thought that the loss of this original render caused much of the later damp problems which emerged in the walls of the church.

It was decided to re-point the exterior masonry in its entirety – an expensive and time-consuming job – but the result looks attractive and should protect the fabric of the building. The lime-mortar pointing sits well with the granite stonework. New internal arrangements include the replacement of the library with a ticket office and shop (now wheelchair accessible) and the provision of a café in the south transept. The roof was re-slated and several of the very handsome stained glass windows were repaired by Sheridan Stained Glass in Kilkenny. Most of the internal walls were re-plastered.

For many years, the Maritime Museum was the only museum or tourist attraction in the wider Dun Laoghaire area. Since its foundation in 1941, the Maritime Institute of Ireland set about forming a collection of books, charts, models, paintings, prints and artefacts relating to the maritime history of Ireland, and eventually established a small museum on St Michael's Wharf, overlooking Dun Laoghaire harbour.

The move to the Mariners' Church allowed the museum to acquire and display much larger and more dramatic items – such as the remarkable glass optic from the Baily Lighthouse on Howth Head, and full size boats. The Baily Optic now sits dramatically centre-stage in the chancel area below the East window.

The museum houses a fascinating variety of objects which tell forgotten stories, such as the story of the *Great Eastern*, the largest ship in the world in its time which laid a telegraph cable across the Atlantic from Kerry to Newfoundland. Other displays include the lifeboat service, the Irish Lights, fishing, yachting, the emergency years, Irish Shipping and the mail boat, and passenger links to Britain and beyond.

The National Maritime Museum is run on an entirely voluntary basis, with small grants from the local authority. F.A.S. (the Irish training and employment authority) has played a valuable role over the years in assisting the work of the museum and by maintaining the former church and keeping it open.

Official post-refurbishment opening by President Michael D. Higgins, 5 June 2012 – showing pulpit in situ and Baily Optic

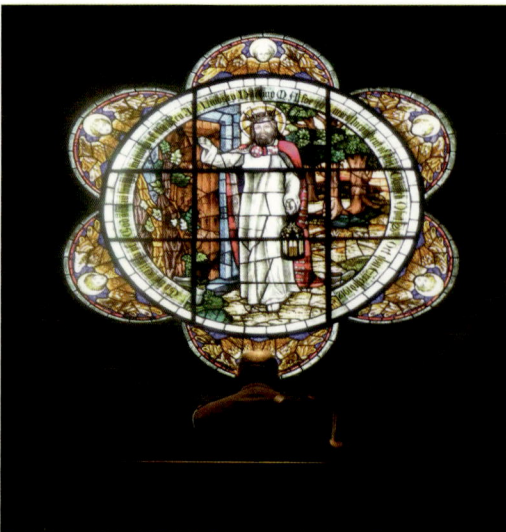

Restored West-end stained glass rose window (Christ as 'Light of the World')

Exhibition space illuminated

Looking from gallery level towards the former chancel

External carved anchor sculptural detail

Other grants have been received from sources such as the Heritage Council and the Department of Environment, but it was direct funding of just under €4million from the Department of An Taoiseach which enabled the most recent works (2005-11) to take place. The National Maritime Museum was able to purchase the building from the R.C.B. in 2011, having up until that point continued to lease it since the 1970s, an arrangement which had entailed various restrictions.

For many years, the museum's continued existence in Dun Laoghaire remained in doubt, as there were conflicting opinions over whether it should move to a much larger site in the Custom House or docks area of Dublin or stay put. Without doubt, the church has limitations in terms of space and expansion, but the museum and the building is of considerable importance to Dun Laoghaire as seaport town. At its official reopening after refurbishment on the 5th June 2012, President of Ireland, Michael D. Higgins – who is patron of The Maritime Institute of Ireland – said, 'This magnificent old Mariners' Church is one of the few large mariner churches in the world. It is a beautiful building … It is great to raise awareness of our maritime heritage.'[4] The use of the Mariners' church as the National Maritime Museum of Ireland for nearly forty years demonstrates how successfully a church can be adapted to a new use, and how an architectural landmark can continue to make a living contribution to a town such as Dun Laoghaire.

| *Peter Pearson*

Notes:
1. Mary Hamilton, *Green and Gold,* 1948
2. R.S. Brooke, *Recollections of an Irish church,* 1877
3. *Belfast Newsletter,* 27 April 1857
4. *Irish Times,* 6 June 2012

Background information
Conservation and refurbishment work, 2005-11:
James Slattery Architect
www.mariner.ie

Christ Church, Church of Ireland, South Main Street, Cork

Triskel Christ Church, Cork

Architectural ensemble of contrasting personalities

Triskel Christ Church provides a music venue and arts centre in the heart of Cork city, amalgamating and physically linking the Triskel Arts Centre, housed in a converted warehouse on Tobin Street, and the adjacent historic Christ Church building. This church, which dates from c. 1726 and is on the site of several past churches going back to the 12th century, had closed as a Church of Ireland place of worship in 1979 after which it became the home of Cork City Archives. Built of white limestone and designed by John Coltsman, the Classical structure with lines of eight oval windows along the lower part of each side elevation, was given a new façade designed by George Richard Pain in 1828 and was further renovated with the introduction of an apse in 1878.[1]

Works in transforming the church to its new purpose for Cork City Council commenced on site in November 2009 and were completed in March 2011. The project was co-funded by Cork City Council and EU Structural funds programme 2007-2013 which is co-funded by the Irish Government and the European Union. Cork City Council was awarded €2.18m under the NSS Gateways & Hubs ERDF grant scheme towards the €4.8m refurbishment costs.

Among the more challenging tests for conservation architecture can be to achieve a satisfactory resolution where combining two historic buildings of radically different architectural style and which are also of distinct architectural value. The expansion of the Triskel in Cork, from its original former warehouse building to incorporate the adjacent, freestanding early 18th-century Christ Church, was one such challenge. In addition to the immediate architectural issues involved in making a coherent architectural ensemble out of two contrasting 'personalities', were the archaeological sensitivities of the National Monument status of Christ Church, and in particular the extent and location of burials immediately around and within the former church; the imperative to reconcile the varying level differences between

Auditorium viewed from first floor gallery, showing new stage within 19th-century apse

all internal floor levels and at street/external level and, not least, the genuinely traumatic and sad implications of the sudden closing of the project architects Murray O'Laoire. Withstanding and rising to all of these was the heroic project architect Helen Devitt, who, through the agency and support of Cork City Council, delivered the project through to completion. Every so often one encounters a completed project where you are reminded of the diverse range of skills required of architects and the Triskel at Christ Church is one of these.

The principal architectural intervention is a narrow circulation and back of house accommodation spine which has been slotted into the tight alleyway which ran between the original Triskel and John Coltsman's fine church of 1718, linking South Main Street and Grand Parade. The appropriation of this open route not only provides the connection between the two existing buildings, but enables the retention and presentation to good effect of the fine spaces within the historic buildings – in particular the Wren-influenced galleried interior volume of Christ Church. To do this, the new insert works hard: its slim girth accommodates lift, stairs, toilets, changing rooms and green room (which through clever planning serves both the retained, well loved, original auditorium and the new venue within the former church). Like the proverbial swan, however, the 'workings' are well concealed, tucked back behind the lift and so leaving a calm, open space around the main circulating stairs which also acts as spill out and concourse space for the many activities within the arts centre. The use here of richly finished timbers - carefully selected to complement the panelling within the church - adds a warmth and intimacy to this space, which, had it otherwise been given the somewhat clichéd minimalist 'high contrast' treatment often applied in these situations, might have resulted in a space less comfortable to linger in.

South elevation showing new storm glazing to restored lead windows

First floor glazed link showing restored 19th-century timber sash church windows

Ground floor foyer, linking the original Triskel building to the new auditorium

The handling of new elements within the historic parts displays a confidence and care which can only come from inquiry, research and ongoing questioning. A good example of this is the treatment of new fire screens within the nave of the former church space. These conform to the existing ordering and proportional systems, while holding back on any decorative expression, so that there is overall coherence but also clarity between new and historic layers. With such an approach the architect displays an understanding of the principles and philosophies of conservation and uses these as a touchstone for creative departure and engagement.

Historic fabric has been given equally careful attention to the new interventions, the principal challenge here being remedial stabilisation works necessary to address the dual complexities of the graveyard within the marsh on which Christ Church was built. This solution is mostly hidden – a neat frame of ties, which span width and length within the roof space – assisted by strapping of the curved (later addition) apsed end to the chancel. Another significant demand was the requirement to provide fire protection of the fabric of Christ Church – a building of national architectural heritage importance – to a level which well exceeded that necessary for normal fire safety. This came as a late requirement and necessitated large bespoke timber and glass screens to fit neatly (and tightly) between the arched and oval windows of the historic building and the new connecting spine.

Section

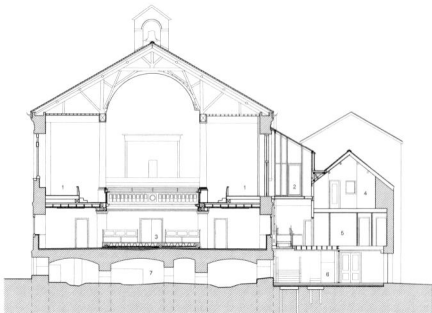

1. First floor gallery /
   exhibition space
2. Glazed link
3. Christ Church auditorium
4. The Black Mariah gallery
5. Toilets
6. Foyer
7. Crypt

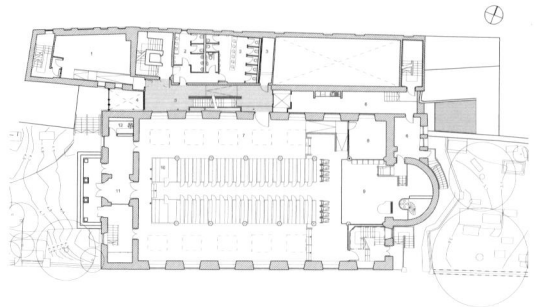

Ground floor plan

1. Plug'd Records
2. Toilets
3. Projection room
4. Double height over side entrance
5. Glazed link
6. Green room
7. Christ Church auditorium
8. 1878 Thomas Lewis pipe organ
9. Stage
10. Sound booth
11. Main entrance foyer
12. Box office

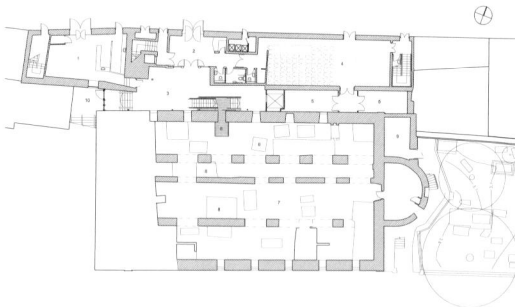

Lower ground floor plan

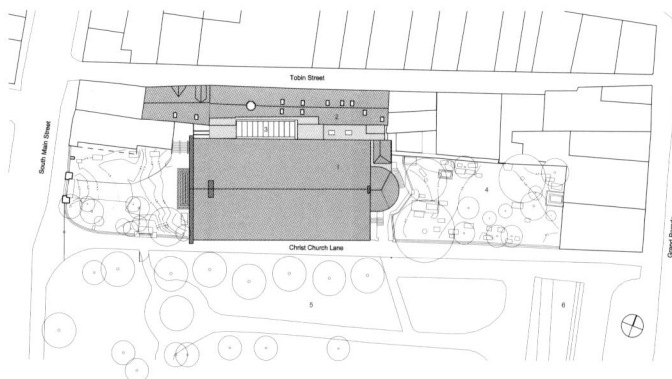

1. Café / Bar
2. Entrance via Tobin Street
3. Foyer
4. Auditorium / Theatre workshop
5. Storage
6. Crypt viewing box
7. Crypt
8. Burials
9. Plant
10. Entrance via glazed link

Site plan

The original mayoral throne commands views of the entire auditorium

There are many tests which measure the success or otherwise when extending an historic building – or in this more unusual case, when connecting two existing historic buildings by adding a third. An overall architectural coherence and legibility is an important one, another is how well the result meets functional and operational objectives and standards. And, certainly for public buildings, the 'humanising' character of the place, as created through the architecture – i.e., the way in which a place is welcoming and truly accessible – is becoming an increasingly important architectural imperative. All these have been delightfully met at the Triskel.

| *Grainne Shaffrey*

Note:
1. Peter Murray provides a useful and detailed historical account of the building in 'Triskel Christchurch', *Irish Arts Review*, Autumn 2011, pp.120-123.

Background Information
Architects: Murray O'Laoire Architects, 2007-2010 (Project Director: Oisin Creagh, Project Architect: Helen Devitt) and Cork City Council, 2010-2011 (Project Architect: Helen Devitt)

http://triskelartscentre.ie

This article largely draws on one which was originally published in a special 'Conservation and Adaptation' edition of the R.I.A.I. journal *Architecture Ireland*, volume 260. It is used with permission; with thanks to the author, R.I.A.I./ *Architecture Ireland*, and the photographer, Helen Devitt (Project Architect).

Holy Trinity, Church of Ireland, Carlingford, Co. Louth

Carlingford Heritage Centre
Retaining essential qualities

Carlingford is a small but historically significant town, located in a wonderful natural setting along Carlingford Lough and between the Cooley and Mourne Mountains. Its distinctiveness is further strengthened by its medieval buildings, many still clearly dominant features in the local townscape, the early Norman castle, 'King John's'; the remains of a Dominican Abbey and, within the town centre, Taaffes Castle; The Tholsel; The Mint and fragments of the medieval town walls.

Carlingford developed in a major fashion during the 19th century. The harbour walls were built, providing better facilities for the local fishing community. The development of Greenore, a few miles along the lough as a steam packet port, provided direct access to the north of England and acted as a stimulus to Carlingford. Many of the attractive buildings on the main street date from this period. The railway connection to Greenore disconnected the castle from the medieval centre and this is still clearly evident today.

There is a strong community ethos in Carlingford, and the inhabitants are fully aware of the town's historic importance. The protection of the local environment is, therefore, an important element in community activities. Carlingford has been for many years fully committed to the aims and objective of the National Tidy Towns Competition. It has won many awards, including the national award in 1988. Because of its setting and historic character, tourism is now an important element in the town's economy. Its location, midway between the main urban centres of Belfast and Dublin, is a help in this regard, and in addition to its historic qualities, Carlingford is also a centre for a variety of adventure sports.

Holy Trinity Church was originally the medieval parish church of Carlingford with a foundation going back to the 15th century, a remnant of which is the West tower, still an important feature of the church

Historic photo of church interior, c.1970

*Exterior view of East window and gable
before restoration*

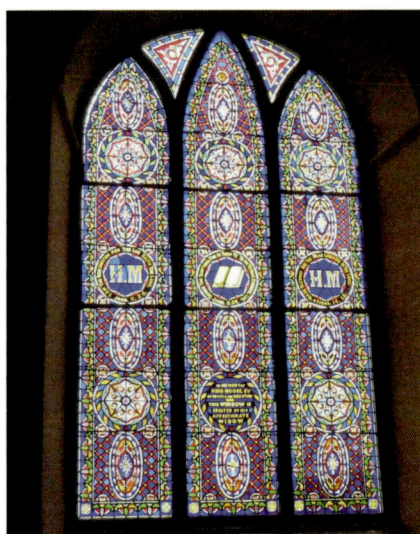

East window after restoration

today. (The church may have been built on the remains of an earlier Norman motte and bailey, and so has predated King John's Castle at the northern end of the town.)

Following on from the Reformation, the dissolution of the monasteries and subsequent Ulster Plantation, the Church of Ireland continued to use the existing churches and this was likely to be the case in Carlingford. According to church records, the building, in a somewhat ruinous state, was repaired during the 17th century. In 1744 the parish church was dedicated to the Holy Trinity.

Holy Trinity Church was extensively rebuilt around 1820, in a 'First Fruits' tradition and became as we know it today, retaining the medieval West tower and a 17th-century door case. It is a simple building with a 5-bay nave, Y-traceried windows, a fine triple light East window, slated roof and plastered walls. The church together with the adjacent graveyard and enclosing stone wall has and still forms an important architectural, historic and aesthetic feature in the centre of Carlingford.

Like many other Church of Ireland churches, it closed for worship in the 1970s and lay empty for a number of years. However, in a town like Carlingford, with a strong community interest in its history, it was never likely to be allowed to fall into total abandonment and dereliction which happened to so many rural churches.

In the 1990s the church was leased to Carlingford Lough Heritage Trust for use as a community centre. Having lain empty for many years, it was, however, in need of major restoration. The distinguished local architect Fergus Flynn Rogers

Mural above and surrounding main internal door

was commissioned to oversee its conversion. It is particularly appropriate that an active member of the local committee, in addition to being a concerned conservation architect, together with the many other members of the local community, contributed to the development of the church in its new, but still important community life.

Major architectural elements were carefully restored: roof, walls, plasterwork and windows, including the fine East window, an important feature of the church. The existing timber floor was repaired and discreet under-floor heating was provided. The central aisle is formed with recycled stone tiles and environmentally friendly coir matting. The side vestry which was in a derelict condition was rebuilt and sensitively extended to provide a boiler room and kitchen facilities.

The project in Carlingford is particularly successful and significant: its community use remains, its simple architectural style and historic qualities have been treated with restraint and respect and no major alterations or insertions were carried out; its interior volume, which is so important in old churches, remains. The graveyard, although now closed for burials, together with its enclosing wall have been maintained and presented in a dignified manner.

An important function of all local heritage centres is to inform visitors of the particular history and character of the building both in its past and contemporary context. Holy Trinity Church scores very well in this respect. Relatively unobtrusive and sophisticatedly designed information panels – in the form of free standing triptychs – provide detailed information on both the character and history of the church but also Carlingford and its surroundings. Furthermore they can be easily closed when other events are taking place, such as musical recitals and lectures, which help to contribute to the maintenance of the building and the activities of the local heritage group.

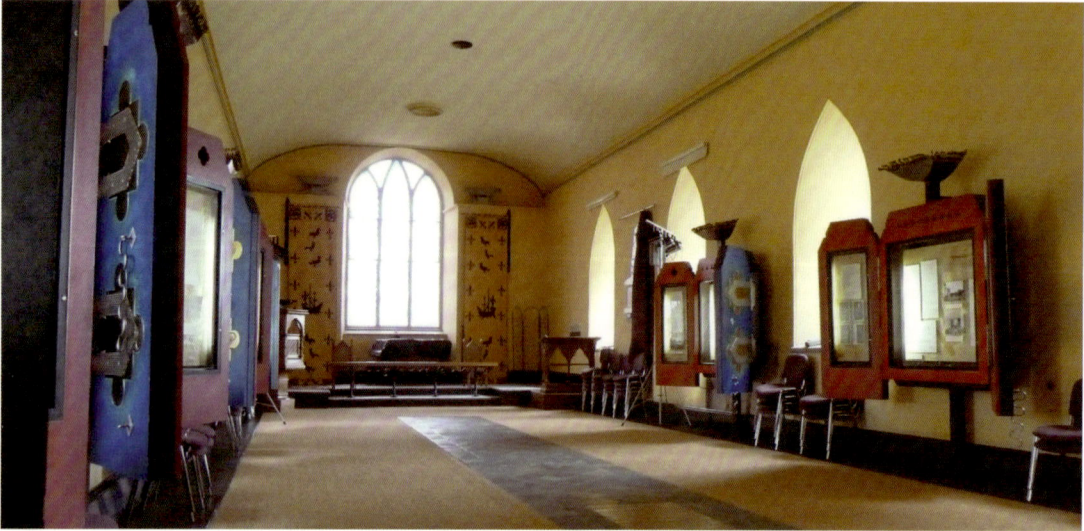

Church interior following restoration

Triptych with panels closed

Triptych opened displaying information panels

Graveyard

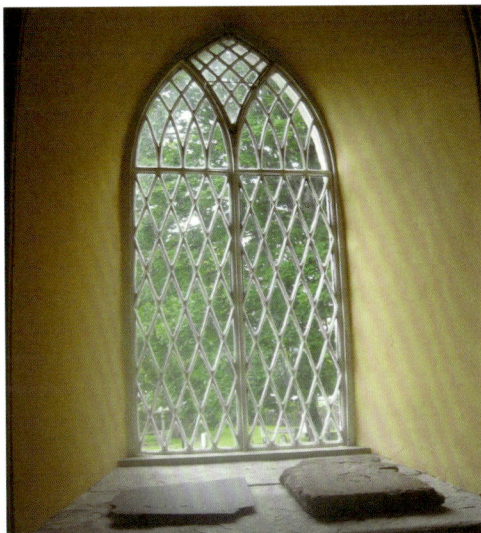

Window after restoration

The historic character of the graveyard has been faithfully retained. There is a wide variety of tombstones ranging from simple stones scattered around on the grass to more elaborate monuments built for important families and individuals. Overall presentation is simple and respectful. The gravel paths are retained, while simple paths of paving stones provide ease of access. There are no intrusions for on-site car parking – all visitors arrive on foot and in doing so experience the distinctive qualities and special personality of the place.

Holy Trinity Church Carlingford provides a good example of how to reuse old buildings without diminishing their essential qualities, and in addition giving the 'new use' a distinctive setting.

| *Patrick Shaffrey*

Background Information
Architect: Fergus Flynn Rogers

www.carlingfordheritagecentre.com

St Peter's, Church of Ireland, North Main Street, Cork

Cork Vision Centre

Visionary rescue

St Peter's is the second of the parish churches of Norman origin in the island city of Cork. It is set back from the line of the street as the valuable street frontage would have contained houses in medieval times but today a small railed churchyard fills the space forming a picturesque interlude along the otherwise busy North Main Street. The medieval church was badly damaged during the 1690 bombardment of the city by Williamite forces and the present building was largely rebuilt between 1785 and 1788. The architect was probably James Hacket who later provided designs for completing the steeple although the battlemented octagonal tower was not completed until 1837. St Peter's, along with many other city-centre Church of Ireland churches in Cork, saw its local congregation diminish through the 20th century and in 1949 it finally closed its doors. The church was subsequently used as a warehouse but by the mid 1990s the building was abandoned and advancing speedily to dilapidation.

Rescue of St Peter's came in the form of a part EU-funded urban renewal project by Cork Corporation (now Cork City Council). Known as the Historic Centre Action Plan, the initiative targeted the adaptation and reuse of buildings in the medieval core of the city as well as enhancement of the public realm in the old medieval heart of the city. St Peter's, having been acquired by Cork Corporation, was identified as a key focal point to the plan, given its visual prominence in the streetscape as well as its historical significance. It was decided to adapt it to serve as a 'Vision Centre', highlighting a range of local and European urban renewal projects and architectural initiatives in a living historic city rather than the more conventional straightforward 'heritage centre'.

By the time the church was acquired, the condition of the building had deteriorated considerably with extensive water damage and various structural problems. In addition, most of the interior ecclesiastical fittings such as the pews, pulpit and altar had long been removed. St Peter's was a typical Georgian auditory chapel, being a regular oblong box with a gallery at one end and tall high-level plainly glazed windows. Surviving historic features included the coved ceiling and dentil cornice, Corinthian pilasters

Gallery space with free-standing display walls

flanking the East window and a small number of memorials, of which the most important is that to Sir Matthew Deane who died in 1710. This stands in the former vestry room adjoining the tower and consists of a large monument with life-size statues commemorating Deane and his wife framed by Corinthian columns. With the church fittings removed, however, the building by and large provided a blank canvas for the City Architect's Department which took charge of the renovation of the building.

Essentially the refurbishment of the former church, which was completed in June 1998, comprised the consolidation and repair of the historic shell of the building and the installation of a cleanly-defined mezzanine structure within it to accommodate new services. The roof was repaired and re-slated while the walls were structurally consolidated before being re-rendered and finished with a distinctive burnt-Sienna pigmented paint. Internally, the ceiling and cornice was repaired and replicated where necessary, the walls were re-plastered and minor repairs were undertaken to the surviving architectural features such as memorials and the East window surround. One feature which was not retained was the organ gallery which was structurally unsound and considered not capable of effective repair and adaptation.

A new polished concrete floor was laid throughout the interior in place of the existing concrete floor installed while the building was a warehouse. The advantage of the new floor is that it incorporates under-floor heating which is one of the most cost-effective and comfortable means of heating such tall interiors. The major new intervention within the interior was the construction of a steel-framed mezzanine structure containing at the lower level a reception desk, internal office, kitchenette and a book shop, and on the upper level an open plan multi-functional space served by a platform lift for wheelchair access and two staircases to ensure compliance with fire safety requirements. This structure is cleanly designed and free-standing of the external walls ensuring legibility as an intervention and lightness in its physical impact. The other major installation and ultimately the biggest attraction in the Vision Centre is an intricately detailed 1:500 scaled topographical model of the city stretching from Blackrock Castle to the Lee Fields.

Reception area with new mezzanine
structure above

Topographical model of Cork city

St Peter's currently operates largely as an exhibition venue. It is managed by Cork Civic Trust, funded by Cork City Council and is open to the public five days per week. A busy schedule of exhibitions is held each year addressing a wide range of topics from architectural design, urban renewal through to contemporary art in all its forms and various worldwide humanitarian and socially conscious issues. St Peter's is also used for performances, film previews and recitals while the building can also be hired for events such as product launches, workshops and seminars as well as, most recently, civil wedding ceremonies.

It is always a delicate – and often very difficult – balance when securing a viable new future for a former place of worship to provide adaptable and flexible space while conserving historic and architecturally distinguished fabric. In the case of St Peter's it is true to say that the previous removal of the internal ecclesiastical fittings and seating during its time as a warehouse provided an unusually flexible open space – a shell within which large-scale exhibitions could be housed; however, it came at the expense of losing some of the architectural and historic detail. This has been compensated for in large measure by sensitive conservation, light-touch new interventions, the restoration of plasterwork and memorials and ultimately saving the overall structure for a contemporary civic purpose.

The conversion of St Peter's to the Vision Centre received Ireland's highest award for conservation, the R.I.A.I. Silver Medal for Restoration 1996-1998. In 2002, the Vision Centre received the Irish American Cultural Award from President McAleese for its own activities.

| Frank Keohane

Background Information
www.corkvisioncentre.com

St Mullin's, Co. Carlow

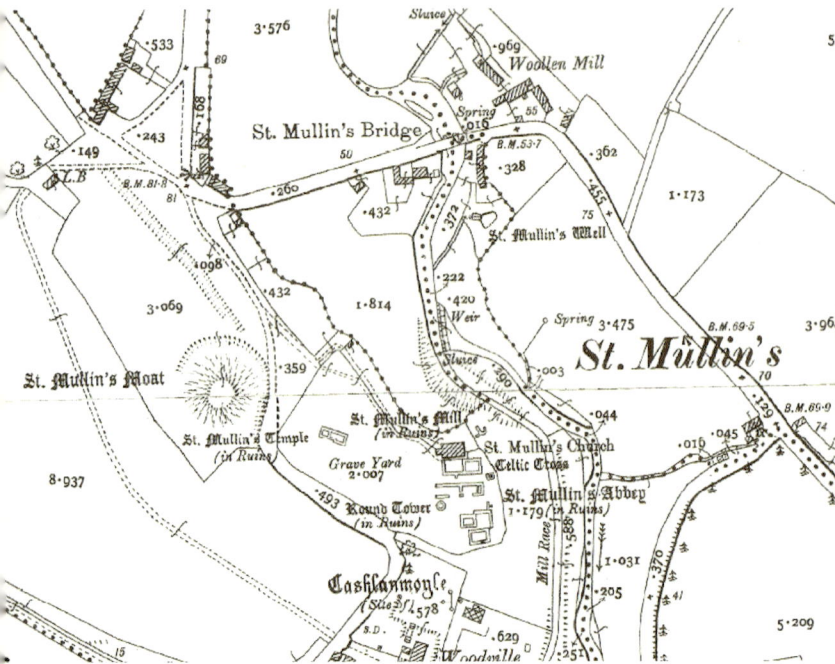

Tower of the former Church of Ireland church

In a beautiful location, at the confluence of the Barrow and Augavaud rivers and beside an early ecclesiastical site and medieval settlement, sits the former Church of Ireland parish church of St Mullin. It was erected in 1811 just beside An Teampall Mor (the great church); this is the oldest church on the site – the gable end of the nave dates from c.1000. Alongside there is a later church on the same east-west axis, the nave of which was converted to a residence in the 16th century. Nearby is a small oratory, dedicated to St James, the base of a round tower and a granite high cross which probably dates from the ninth century. Within the graveyard there are structures and memorials as well as headstones with 18th- and 19th-century dates and many more modern ones.

The present approach to the graveyard is dominated by a large motte and bailey erected by the Anglo–Normans in the 12th century. St. Moling's well, which resembles a small early stone church, is outside the graveyard and further down the hill towards the later mill buildings by the Aughavaud River. St Moling who was responsible for building the monastery at St Mullin's in the 7th century excavated a watercourse and erected a cornmill for the use of the community. This prince, poet and priest is also said to have started a ferry service across the River Barrow on a locally constructed raft. The Book of Moling dating from the late 8th century is in Trinity College Library and the ornamental metal shrine made for the pocket gospel-book in 1402 is in the National Museum of Ireland.

Aerial view of St Mullin's

Model of church

Norman motte

Vicar: Canon Hay, c.1910

The churches

Rev. C. McCollum, Thelma Cantlon and Rev. Fr E. Aughney, 28 August 2011

Wall monuments

Wall monuments and display

The former Church of Ireland church, built with a grant of £800 from the Board of First Fruits, apparently had a small congregation. Historically the church was associated with the McMurrough Kavanagh family of Borris House; more recent family associations were with the Odlum family. After 1967, when the nearby Odlum Flour mill closed, services in the church became infrequent. At an ecumenical service in 1980 members of the Odlum family were present and the last person who was baptised in the church.

In 1986, St Mullin's Muintir na Tire acquired the church for the purposes of creating a heritage centre.[1] Its location in such a picturesque riverside setting alongside the archaeological site with later industrial heritage nearby makes it an ideal area for recreational walking and nature exploration. Inside the church there is a sophisticated exhibition and display which was designed and erected by fourth-year architecture students from University College Dublin in 2010. This allows artefacts to be displayed and local crafts and customs to be explained. The exhibition includes models as well as genealogical information and is arranged in a linear fashion on an east-west axis. The memorials along the south wall form a backdrop to it.

A visit to St Mullin's is an unforgettable experience – somehow it feels as if one has stepped into a complete distillation of Irish history on a single stunning site. The vision of Muintir na Tire in acquiring the church as a heritage centre combined with the knowledge, enthusiasm and commitment of the local community in keeping their heritage alive is exemplary.

| *Primrose Wilson*

Note:
1. Information provided to the author by Bridie Lawlor, Curator, St Mullin's Heritage Centre. Useful information on the St Mullin's site includes: *St Mullin's – Archaeology Ireland Heritage Guide No.5* (March 1999), and O'Neill, M. & Lawlor, B., *Heritage Trail St Mullin's, Co Carlow* (1996)

Background Information
http://stmullinsheritagecentre.com

Teach Cheoil

Traditional music in churches in West Clare

St Andrew's, Ennistymon

It is a delightful concept that 'Architecture is music in space, as it were a frozen music'[1] and appears to be a particularly apt parallel to draw with ecclesiastical buildings. Music plays a central part in the worship of many denominations but in particular in the Anglican tradition. So it seems fitting that two former Church of Ireland churches in County Clare have been converted for the enjoyment of traditional music. In 1986 Comhaltas Ceoltóirí Eireann converted St Andrew's to Teach Ceoil (house of music) Ennistymon, and in 1995 St Senan's Church became Teach Ceoil Kilrush.[2]

St Andrew's, Ennistymon, was built in 1830 on a prominent site. Services were held in the church until it closed in the1970s and in 1986 it was acquired by Comhaltas for use as a cultural centre. The setting of the exterior has been carefully retained; its graveyard is well tended and a discreet extension was added to the rear. The interior of the building has been adapted for its new use and the pulpit and wall memorials carefully retained. The church with its pinnacles and crenellated octagonal bell tower dramatically closing the vista at the top of Church Street, Ennistymon, is a truly memorable sight and a superb piece of townscape.

St Senan's, Kilrush, was erected in 1813 with a grant from the Board of First Fruits; a tower was added c.1840. It is a single cell structure with a tall crenellated tower and pointed arch windows with attractive cast-iron quarry glazing. An agreement was reached with the local community in 1995, after it became redundant, for its reuse by Comhaltas. New facilities, including a small café and lavatories, have been inserted within the shell of the building and the windows, including the stained glass, and wall monuments carefully restored and retained. The 19th-century wall memorials to the Vandeleur family are by Thomas Kirk R.H.A. and are important artefacts.[3]

St Senan's, Kilrush

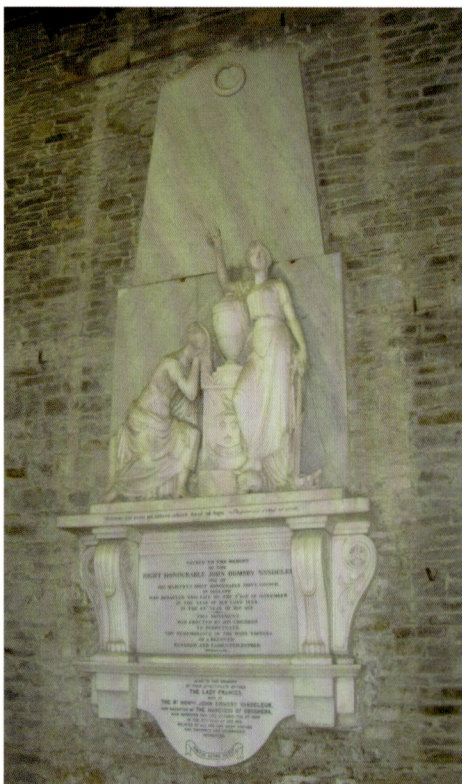

John Ormsby Vandeleur memorial, St Senan's

Seymour Vandeleur memorial, St Senan's

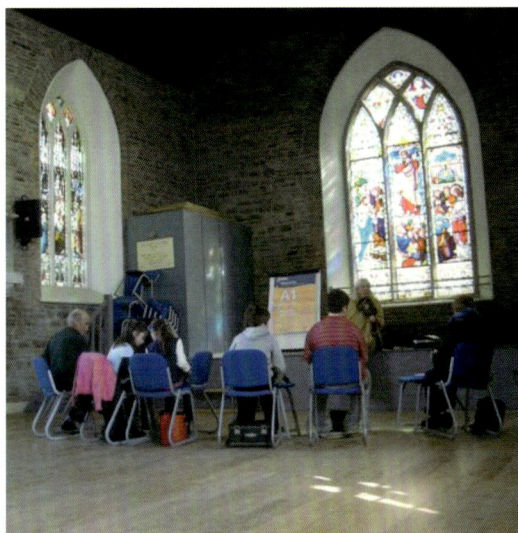

Traditional music class

Vandeleur mausoleum, Kilrush

O'Doherty grave, Kilrush

The graveyard has many interesting grave monuments; several men are buried there who died when the steamship Europa, bound for Foynes, was torpedoed by a German submarine at the mouth of the Shannon in October 1918.

Comhaltas Ceoltóirí Eireann was formed in 1951 to promote Irish traditional music and to encourage the hundreds of traditional musicians in the country who were not always appreciated in social and intellectual circles. Every year they organise a Fleadh Cheoil, a great annual festival of Irish traditional music, song and dance, attended by enthusiasts and the cream of traditional Irish musicians. The aim of the Fleadh is to promote traditional music and to arrest the decline in its popularity. Comhaltas is a cultural organisation with many branches in Ireland, Britain and worldwide.

It is greatly to the credit of Comhaltas Ceoltóirí that they have converted these churches and brought them alive again for the enjoyment and teaching of traditional music in County Clare. The retention of these locally important ecclesiastical buildings and their use by the community ensures that part of the material history of the county is retained and used for the benefit of all.

| *Primrose Wilson*

Notes:
1. Friedrich Wilhelm Joseph von Schelling, *Philosophy of Art*
2. See: *An introduction to the architectural heritage of County Clare* (N.I.A.H., 2009)
3. See: Homan Potterton, *Irish church monuments 1570-1880* (Belfast, 1975)

Roscommon

A tale of two converted churches in the Square, Roscommon

Former Presbyterian church and manse

Historic view of the church and manse

Former Catholic church

The town of Roscommon offers an interesting example of how church buildings can be successfully and imaginatively reused once ecclesiastical purposes have been served. The reuse of such architecturally significant churches allows for their continued presence to be felt within a townscape with no loss of dignity and a very strong contribution made to local civic space. In Roscommon two such buildings are situated in the central public thoroughfare.

The former Presbyterian church and manse form an interesting and significant architectural set piece in the Square. The buildings are set back from the street line and fine chamfered cut stone gate piers, cast-iron gates and railings enhance the setting of the composition.

The Presbyterian congregation was established c. 1863.[1] The church, funded by Michael Sherra, was erected c.1865 and an adjoining plot was purchased in 1871 for the manse. The church has a symmetrical gabled façade of local limestone with simple classical detailing; two tall round-headed windows flank the doorway while above the front door is a raised oculus containing a 'Star of David' window. Local tradition says the window commemorates its Welsh builders but a hexagram also symbolises the Sign of Solomon or the Shield of David.

After amalgamation with the congregation in Athlone, the last resident minister left in 1925 and the manse changed hands several times. The church remained in occasional use until c.1955; however, it closed after the death of the last member of the Watt family of Abbey Street. In 1990 the church was acquired by the Harrison Hall Trust for the use of the local community and as a tourist office and county museum. The building was

Left and right: Interior views of the former Presbyterian church as tourist office and county museum

carefully restored, a discreet extension was added and many features, including the pulpit, retained. Its central location and displays of artefacts of local interest make it an attractive place for visitors to the town to locate information as well as a valued amenity for residents. The adjacent manse is now a restaurant, and the two buildings form a striking group. It is to the credit of the local community that they have saved and found a new use for these architecturally significant buildings in an important location in their town.

For over forty years, from 1865 to 1903, Catholics and Presbyterians worshipped side by side in the Square. The fine neo-classical building in the middle of the Square is now in use as a bank but in the past it has served as a Catholic church, market house and court house. In 1762 the Dublin architect George Ensor was commissioned by the Grand Jury to build a court and market house on the site of the earlier session house. When a new court house was built in Abbey Street in 1822, it became redundant.[2] Following Catholic Emancipation in 1829, the building was bought by the Parish Priest, Fr John Madden, and converted into a Catholic church. In 1844, front and rear extensions were added; this altered the orientation of the building from facing the gaol to looking towards the town. The building firmly stamps its authority on its location in the centre of the Square.

The new church of the Sacred Heart built in Abbey Street was consecrated in 1903 and the building, therefore, once again became redundant. It was used for a time as the Harrison Memorial Hall and then purchased by the Bank of Ireland.

The various interim uses of both buildings have preserved an important snapshot of Ireland's architectural heritage as well as providing places of worship for their communities.

| *Primrose Wilson*

Note:
1. *Roscommon Herald Magazine*, vol.4, 1992
2. *An Introduction to the architectural heritage of Roscommon* (N.I.A.H., 2004)

St John's, Knockainey, Co. Limerick
Faithfully conserved

St John's, Knockainey

Exterior, showing separate tower with spire

Exterior view of gable wall

'Old graveyards with a scatter of lichen-encrusted gravestones and trees standing to attention rank amongst the most evocative features of the Irish landscape.'[1] This line could have been written with St John's, Knockainey in mind. The church is also covered in lichen and with its boundary wall and sexton's house nearby creates an attractive and harmonious group. There were churches on this site since medieval times but the most recent was erected in 1861 by the Church of Ireland. The tower and spire are free-standing and belong to an earlier church, built pre 1762.[2] The graveyard contains many interesting graves and mausolea, several resting side by side are grass-covered and barrel-roofed with the door at the end; the undulating effect on the graveyard is stunning.

The church was deconsecrated in 1999 but local people did not want to see it fall into disrepair. Members of the Knockainey Historical & Conservation Society approached Tom Cassidy, Conservation Officer with Limerick County Council, about funding for a conservation report. The local school hosted a concert to raise match funding and interest was raised within the local community. The Society negotiated a five year lease from the Representative Church Body (this was recently extended for a further twenty years) and a candlelight Christmas concert was held in the church.

Just as local interest was concerned with the future of the building the Society met with Ballyhoura Rural Development; they were distributing LEADER funding to assist the regeneration of local

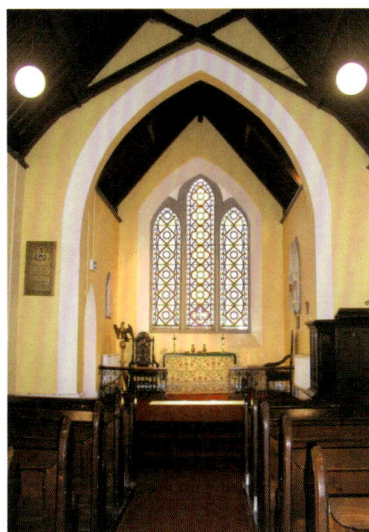

Interior with view to chancel

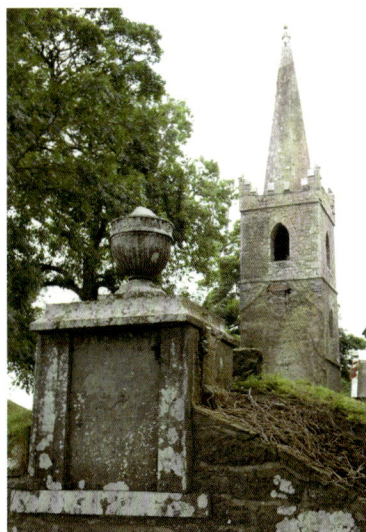

View from graveyard showing memorial, tower and line of old church

Date stone on gable wall

communities. They were very helpful and with assistance from County Council departments and donations from members of the community the Society raised the funds to conserve the church carefully and to put in new heating and lighting. On entering the church today it is just as if a service is about to begin; the sacred ambience remains as wall memorials, pews, pulpit, communion rails and holy table are all in place. The memorials provide important historical information on local families. The atmosphere is warm and welcoming and the Society organises a successful series of concerts and events. The restoration of the former sexton's house provides facilities for performers and audience as well as an office and meeting rooms; this ensures that the graveyard was not disturbed to provide modern amenities.

This project is an exemplary scheme showing community partnership in action. Members of the community who came together after the closure knew the importance of early action and good conservation practice. As the ICOMOS Burra Charter points out 'Conservation work should do as much as necessary, yet as little as possible to the building to ensure its future'.[3] The Society was fortunate to encounter Ballyhoura Rural Development whose funding priorities matched theirs and a helpful County Council. However, most of all it was the resourcefulness and pride of the local community which saved and reused a precious local resource.

| *Primrose Wilson*

Notes:
1. Patrick J. O'Connor, *Some studies of the Irish scene*, Irish Landscape Series no. 2 (1992)
2. N.I.A.H. *An introduction to the architectural heritage of County Limerick* (2011)
3. ICOMOS *Burra Charter* - Article 3.1

Converting Churches into Libraries

Arched entrance to Kilfinaghty, Sixmilebridge

On the hill of Armagh close to St Patrick's cathedral is the Armagh Public Library erected in 1771 and extended in 1848. Over the door is Greek inscription in archaic lettering, the generally accepted interpretation of which is 'the healing place of the soul'.[1] Churches are also places where our souls are refreshed and healed and perhaps this is why redundant churches convert so successfully to libraries. Many churches are centrally located in towns and villages – ideal locations for libraries. If there is a graveyard it provides an oasis of calm green space, and there is usually a convenient space for parking.

Churches play a significant role, locally and nationally, in our spiritual, social and community life and are often the most prominent and ambitious buildings in their locality. By definition they are public buildings cared for by their congregation but they are also the heritage of their communities. There is great sadness when they become redundant but this blow is softened when a benign community use is found for the building. Churches converted to libraries provide a pleasant and welcoming ambience as well as a good space for reading and study. Mobile bookstands mean that the space can be flexible and used to hold community events.

It is greatly to the credit of local authorities all around Ireland that they saw the potential of redundant churches and converted a number of them into libraries. The success of the conversion is greatly enhanced when church gates, railings and ancillary buildings are retained in use. In **Gort,** Co. Galway where the cemetery is located beside the former Church of Ireland (now a library) and accessed through the same fine gates the footpaths and discreet directional signage do not intrude on its setting. The Presbyterian

Gort, Co. Galway

Gort, Co. Galway

Gort, Co. Galway

Gort, Co. Galway

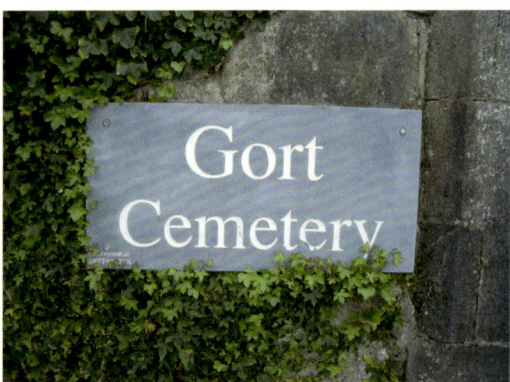

Gort, Co. Galway

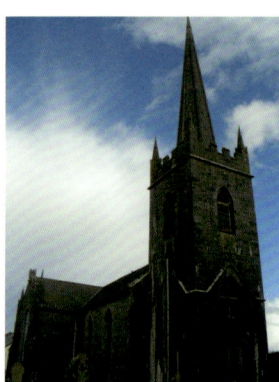

Gort, Co. Galway

Church in **Ennis,** Co. Clare was converted to a
library during European Architectural Heritage Year
(1975) and a large modern building erected to the
rear while the adjoining manse became a local history
library. Though the church is no longer in use as
a library its presence still enhances the streetscape,
masking the extension to the rear while the former
manse contains information of local interest.

The majority of churches converted to libraries can
accommodate storage in galleries, small rooms and
former vestries, but occasionally an extension is
required. In **Garristown,** Co Dublin where a small
church building has been converted to a Carnegie
library, the linear extension blends well with the
surroundings.[2] The former Roman Catholic chapel in
Dunshauglin, Co. Meath is another small building
where discreet extensions have been added to the rear.
In **Oranmore,** Co. Galway two of the galleries of the
original T-plan church were retained and one is used
for storage while another is converted to a meeting
room; in other libraries small rooms were discreetly

Ennis, Co. Clare

Garristown, Co. Dublin

Dunshaughlin, Co. Meath

Garristown, Co. Dublin

Oranmore, Co. Galway

Oranmore, Co. Galway c.1970

Ballinrobe, Co. Mayo

Oranmore, Co. Galway, 2012

converted into offices and small kitchens for the use of staff.

The treatment of the interior space is never easy but where the original architectural design, plan form and spatial volume can be read most successfully is when east-west orientation remains and the space is not permanently subdivided. Where the height of the bookcases is not above eye level (and this is usually the case) the original plan form is most easily seen. In several libraries bookstands are arranged on either side of the former aisle which permits ease of access for readers but also retains the original orientation. In **Ballinrobe,** Co. Mayo the use of the original entrance and the terracotta floor tiling in the library recreates the feeling of walking up the aisle of the church. This library also retains the pulpit, lectern and reredos, all memorials and stained glass windows and has a space delineated for group study in the former chancel.

Memorials are often fine examples of calligraphy and beautiful artefacts as well as sources of historical information. The complete set of stained glass windows, donated by different members of the congregation but to the same design pattern, in the former Dunshaughlin chapel provides a sense of coherence to the overall design as well as genealogical information. In library buildings converted from churches the memorials and stained glass windows add a historical dimension as well as providing interest and delight. In the opinion of at least one librarian, stained glass also provides protection for books from UV light.

| *Loughrea, Co. Galway pre-restoration*

| *Loughrea, Co. Galway post-restoration*

| *Loughrea, Co. Galway*

| *Gort, Co. Galway*

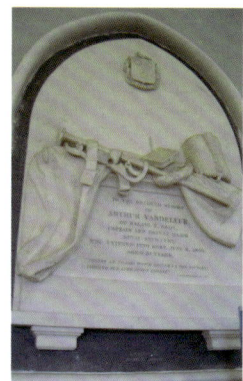
| *Kilfinaghty Co. Clare*

The task of restoration and conversion is more expensive when a church is redundant for some time. Strong local leadership and early decision making about its future can prevent it becoming a target for vandals; some interim maintenance or meanwhile use can ensure that the roof does not suffer from neglect. In **Charleville,** Co. Cork the local authority showed great vision when it converted the redundant Church of Ireland, which was vacant for some time. Unusually this iconic building breaks the street line by being set back from the Main Street; its graveyard provides a green space in the centre of the town. The former Church of Ireland in **Clonaslee,** Co Laois, St Manman's, is an important focal point for the village;

| *Dunshaughlin, Co. Meath*

Clonaslee, Co. Laois

Opening, 1978 L-R: Seamus Keating, County Manager; Most Revd Eamon Casey, Bishop of Galway; Cllr Frank Glynn, Chairman of County Council; Rt Revd Edwin Owen, Bishop of Killaloe and Clonfert; Thomas Sharkey, County Librarian

erected in 1814 it was converted to a heritage centre and then a library. In 2012 the library closed but it remains in use by the local community.

After it was decided to close the Church of Ireland in **Gort,** the bishop, the Right Reverend Edwin Owen, handed over the church to the local community. At the reception in 1972 to mark the handover he said:

> In these days when all our Christian values are under attack, no right-thinking person can be glad to see the representatives of any Christian church tradition disappear from out midst. Churches are very dear to those who have long worshipped in them. They are hallowed by the prayer and worship of generations of good people. They are impregnated with the emotions of these people. Their children were baptised there; they were married here; they began their last journey here. Those responsible for such buildings must be careful as to how they dispose of them. They could be demolished, or sold or left to become a ruin of doubtful charm. It is here that the gladness of today shines out. In these days we are coming to see that worship is more than a church service … It is with this idea in mind that we have decided the future of this church. It is at the disposal of your diocesan trustees for such religious and cultural purposes as you may think seemly and proper. If it is used in this way then far from its life being ended, it is having a new birth.[3]

In his response, the Roman Catholic bishop, the Most Reverend Dr Browne, said he was 'moved by the magnanimity' of the decision to hand it over to the Catholic community. He added, 'it was a very wise and a very Christian decision. Your church in Gort was of particular interest because it was surrounded by a cemetery where Catholics and Protestants were buried. We accept it as a sacred gift and also as a sign of the fraternity which existed for so many years in Gort between the religious communities.' In 1978 the building opened as a library.

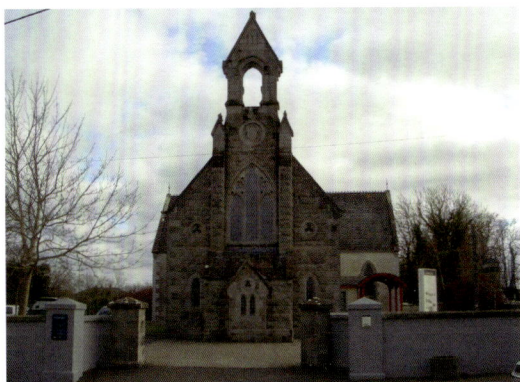

Dunshaughlin, Co. Meath

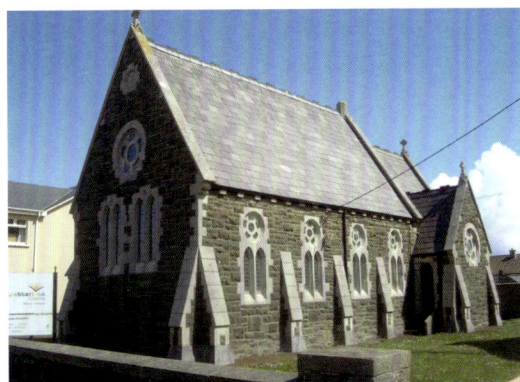

Ballybunion, Co Kerry

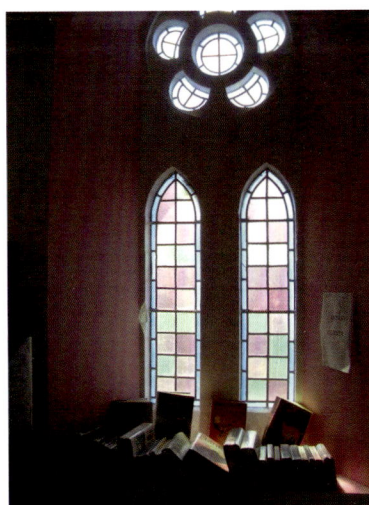

Ballybunion, Co Kerry

The stories of the heroic efforts of local groups to retain their former places of worship in use deserves to be told just as much as the people whose memorials grace their walls. The chapel at Oranmore was erected c.1800 after considerable fund-raising and then the roof blew off in the Big Wind of January 1839. The parish priest went to America and raised the funds to repair the roof; the building served its community until c.1970 when it was deemed to be too small for its congregation. The church was saved from demolition by the valiant efforts of the local community and restored through a F.A.S. (Irish training and employment authority) training scheme. In 2000 the building was handed over to Galway County Council and opened as a library.

The local community and Clare County Council worked together to restore and reuse the former Church of Ireland in **Sixmilebridge** (dating from 1810, with a good three-stage tower) and to turn it into Kilfinaghty Public Library. The amazing story of the fund-raising and determination of the local community is told on their website www.clarelibrary.ie. This is a church conversion much enhanced by the well maintained graveyard and the retention of the encircling wall, stone steps and archway.

Churches are iconic structures which not only add great value to our urban and rural architectural heritage, but, as these examples have demonstrated, retain real social and cultural importance in their localities. The successful conversion of those which have become libraries enables them to continue to fulfil both of these roles well.

| *Primrose Wilson*

Notes:
1. McKinstry et al, *The buildings of Armagh,* Belfast, 1992
2. Brendan Grimes, *Irish Carnegie Libraries,* Dublin, 1998
3. St Joseph's Secondary School, Gort, - project awarded a High Commendation in the Sir Graham Larmor Award1977

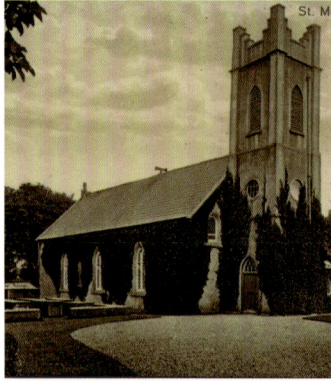
Ballinrobe, Co. Mayo c.1910

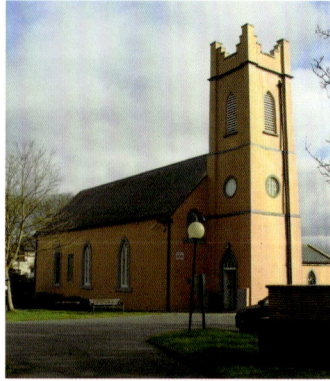
Ballinrobe, Co, Mayo, 2012

Claremorris, Co.Mayo c.1910

Claremorris, Co. Mayo 2012

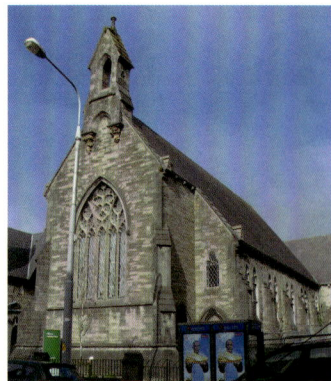
Sligo, Co. Sligo

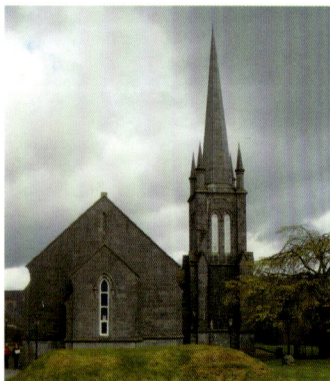
Charleville, Co. Cork

Selection of churches converted to libraries:

Ballinrobe, Co. Mayo
(formerly Church of Ireland)

Ballybunion, Co. Kerry
(formerly Church of Ireland)

Buncrana, Co. Donegal
(formerly Presbyterian)

Charleville, Co. Cork
(formerly Church of Ireland)

Claremorris, Co. Mayo
(formerly Church of Ireland)

Clonaslee, Co. Laois
(formerly Church of Ireland)

Dunshaughlin, Co. Meath
(formerly Roman Catholic)

Ennis, Co. Clare
(formerly Presbyterian)

Garristown, Co. Meath
(formerly Roman Catholic)

Gort, Co. Galway
(formerly Church of Ireland)

Kilfinaghty, Sixmilebridge, Co. Clare
(formerly Church of Ireland)

Loughrea, Co. Galway
(formerly Church of Ireland)

Oranmore, Co. Galway
(formerly Roman Catholic)

Rush, Co. Dublin
(formerly Roman Catholic)

Sligo, Co. Sligo
(former Presbyterian Church)

Work in Progress

Portaferry Presbyterian Church
Arcadia in the Ards

In 1840 the then large Presbyterian congregation of Portaferry engaged the young Ulster architect John Millar to design a new church. The previous building was a plain T-shaped barn which had suffered severe damage in the great storm of 1839. For many years the Presbyterian incumbents had, in succession, run a Classics School. Whether it was this that led to the erection of a Greek Revival temple or a simple desire to have an edifice that personified the congregation's social aspirations, is unknown – the sadly unminuted Session and Committee meetings must have been interesting occasions.

The new church was built on the site of the old. Millar's take on a Greek temple is, of course, unique.[1] His sources are unknown but it is thought that the building is modelled on the Temple of Nemesis on the island of Rhamnos. The Society of the Dilettante had published various volumes of architectural drawings and conjectures – the Temple of Nemesis was certainly largely conjecture as little of it exists save for a few broken columns and some foundations. Millar had to fit the temple onto a steep slope: thus at the North end the building has a hexastyle Doric portico resting at almost ground level (the entrance to the gallery) whilst at the South end it has a hexastyle Doric portico on a high podium which gives entrance to the ground floor. The link to the Temple of Nemesis is most clearly articulated in the columns, amongst the first in the British Isles to make use of entasis, which are fluted only at the base and just under the capitals but otherwise plain – exactly as on Rhamnos. Cleverly, somewhat incongruously and probably totally originally, Millar provided an infill between the four central columns at each end to create vestibules, glazing the infill with cast iron windows. The only identified historical precedent is Schinkel's unexecuted plans for the Neue Wache in Berlin. We will never know if this was Millar's inspiration. The original temple had columns on all four sides whilst Portaferry only has them at each end, Millar creating deep thin windows on the long sides – an echo of those original but absent columns?

Internally, Millar ingeniously created seating for 500. The pews retain their doors, the congregation having steadfastly resisted any attempts to modernise. The ground floor pews have mini-sarcophagi capping their ends whilst upstairs he used large roundels, producing soldier-like ranks of seating. The roundels reflect the Bassaen capitals of the internal columns which support a handsomely coffered ceiling. The interior is architecturally symmetrical, though much of the impact of the pilasters and columns is lost by the liberal application of beige paint. At the front of the church the central portion of wall was replaced with the 1917 organ case facade which creeps out around the central columns.
The church is largely unaltered except for the installation of the organ; two stained glass First World War windows; heating and electric light (and perhaps not as much of either as those today might like); and the removal of pews from the front of the church to create a choir box. The original Georgian glazed

Interior looking towards the pulpit and organ from the gallery

windows along the sides were replaced with Art Deco glass in the 1930s which, as is typical of the style, cast a slightly dismal hue over the building's interior.

Things have changed for the congregation since the 1840s: the Famine, emigration, agricultural depressions and two world wars have taken a heavy toll but today it stands at 60 families, 150 souls and an average attendance of 30. The building was almost forgotten, languishing in a side street in a sea of tarmac car parks. Huge repair bills loomed and it is hard for a small congregation to justify such expenditure to maintain a building used once a week for an hour. Otherwise, it is secured behind locked gates and high railings but these of course have not deterred glue-sniffers, covert smokers and/or disciples of Banksie, though it is possible that a policy of much more open access might?

In 2006 several concerned individuals met to ponder the future for this building. Familiarity, and its associated contempt, had blinkered most of us into thinking that, like most of us, it was probably beyond redemption. Contrary to perceived wisdom we would argue that this is a good place to start – no rose tinted lenses. We realised that one of the congregation's best assets is the building – a building that a few architectural cognoscenti rated rather highly, albeit in rather obscure publications, but one of which few members of the general public were even aware. Somewhat unremarkably the building had been listed B+. We, as complete novices – a farmer, a farmer's wife, a retired teacher, a retired accountant, a civil servant and a medical man, set ourselves the challenge of rejuvenation.

How does one rescue a building especially a building owned by a congregation and managed by an elected committee? The first thing was to define our objectives and then to become formally constituted which we did by establishing the 'friends of Portaferry Presbyterian Church' (fPPC) an entirely secular organisation existing in parallel with the Church Committee – that is with no formal link to the congregation and specifically no statutory representation by any officer of the church on its Board. This

Exterior of church

Detail of Ionic capital

Historic view of exterior

is, of course, potentially a diplomatic minefield but we have been very fortunate to have the support of the Committee and we work very closely with them. Becoming a charity and a limited company not only offers legal protection but is essential for obtaining money from almost every grant funding body. Experienced legal opinion is mandatory as so much can hang on the turn of a phrase in a constitution. This separate status also opens up secular grant funding streams from which churches are usually excluded.

The second phase was to assess just how bad the building's condition was. A conservation architect is key: there is no point in applying a fresh coat of paint over critical cracks. Having determined what needs to be done, finances are next. There is a tradition in churches of financing projects by baking cakes: the value of cakes has not, however, kept pace with building costs and professional fees. In our case we decided that instead of baking cakes we would run international arts events and open the building at every possible opportunity to the general public. Within two years the building was 'on the map'. We don't make significant profits from our concerts: do not make the mistake of thinking that they will fund any restoration, they will not. What they do is raise the building's public profile. We also took soundings from architectural historians who were unanimous in their view that the building should be A-listed. With the Church Committee's blessing we organised a day to celebrate the architecture of the building and invited everyone we could think of. Subsequently, we made our case to the Northern Ireland Environment Agency who reinspected the building and upgraded it to A status. For N.I.E.A. funding it makes no difference whether a building is B+ or A listed but being an A has a cachet that B+ simply does not in applying to other grant funding bodies.

fPPC received a Round 1 Heritage Lottery Fund grant of £40,000 to work up a Round 2 application and 42 applications have been made to other trust funds. Matching funding is a core part of a successful HLF application, including 'in-kind' activities. H.L.F. grants require a significant heritage component: we have developed a programme of exhibitions on the region, a programme of heritage building skills training and a programme dedicated to liturgical music. fPPC engaged Bill Maxwell of Maxwell Pierce as architect for the project in an open competition, and he is drawing up a detailed programme of works to address the main issues.

We are far from having secured our full funding. This is a long process. Our advice at this point? Be properly constituted; determine strengths; determine aims precisely; take professional advice even though it might seem expensive; be creative; make sure you have an up-to-date website (www. friendsppc.org); ask – the worst people can say is NO. We have been astounded at people's generosity with time, advice and skills. Most of all keep your management structure tight and choose your Board carefully: we have a lot of fun in each other's company – you should too.

| *Neil McClure*

Note:
1. For further descriptions of the building, see: C.E.B. Brett, *Buildings of North County Down* (Belfast, 1999), pp.62-3; article by C.E.B. Brett, *Ulster Architect,* Vol.11 No. 9 (1994); and article by Paul Larmour, *Perspective,* Vol. 3 No. 1 (1994)

Background Information
http://friendsppc.org/wordpress

Duncairn Complex, Belfast
Salt & light in North Belfast

The former Duncairn Presbyterian Church stands at the corner of Duncairn Avenue and the Antrim Road. Since the 1960s and over the years of 'the Troubles', the congregation numbers had been dwindling and the decision was taken in 1995 to close Duncairn and combine the congregation with St Enoch's Presbyterian, at nearby Carlisle Circus.

In 1988, the church, manse and boundary walls had been statutorily listed at grade B+ by the Department of the Environment, in recognition of the importance of the whole complex, both architecturally and historically, to the character of the area.

The church had been designed by the architect William Barre (c.1826-1897) who was also noted for the design of the Gothic Revival Unitarian Church in Newry, Co. Down (1852) and responsible for a number of churches in Belfast during the same period. Having secured his first Belfast commission for the Unitarian Church on York Street in 1855, the architect honed his eccentric, eclectic style in the designs for Duncairn Presbyterian Church in 1860. The T-shaped church was designed in High Victorian Gothic Style with a ship-like, hammer beam roof and 'Barre's tower' – allegedly the first of its kind to hang a 'Presbyterian bell'. Local Scrabo sandstone was used to build the church, the school house and manse which were completed in 1862.

Over the next fifty years, various development works were carried out on the site by the architects Young and Mackenzie. That firm added the south aisle and conical stair in 1871 and the manse was extended in 1875. A north aisle was added in 1884, together with a gallery and an organ chamber in 1906. The original School House was demolished and new halls were added in 1914-1915.

The complex was purchased from the church by the 174 Trust in 1995, a trust established by a group of concerned Christians in 1982 to tackle many of the problems confronting the local community. The church buildings initially provided an income from being leased out but as the fabric of the building began suffering serious deterioration from weather damage and vandalism, they have fallen into disuse. The Trust, however, continues to operate from a neighbouring building and wishes to expand its existing programmes and develop work in new areas. Activities as diverse as boxing, after school clubs, community physiotherapy services and Irish Dancing classes have been organised by the Trust and over 800 people continue to use these facilities each year. In order to accommodate its further activities, the church buildings are to be restored and re-utilised.

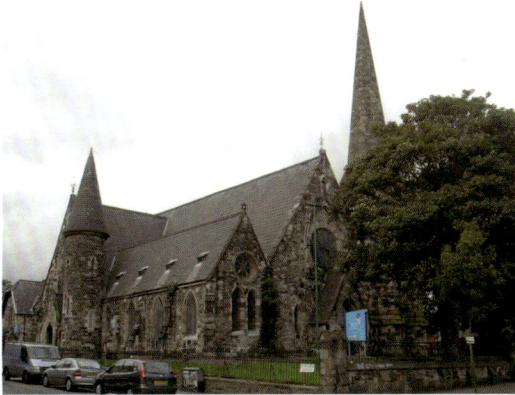

Duncairn church from Antrim Road

Condition of interior (side aisle)

Condition of interior (main aisle)

The reuse project has three sources of funding. Heritage Lottery Fund and International Fund for Ireland grants have been awarded to the 174 Trust, together with anticipated N.I.E.A. grant aid, to restore the former church and transform it into a centre for arts, culture and heritage. Following its restoration the building will be used as the venue for an ambitious programme of community-focused events and activities, complementing other activity on the site and allowing an expansion of cross community co-operation. Doherty Architects has drawn up a scheme which will restore the historic fabric of the church building whilst linking it to the halls and manse. Extensive conservation works will be needed to preserve the building and works will include repairs to the Scrabo Stone exterior, the roof and floors and reusing existing materials where possible.

The restored building will provide a new welcome area, tourist information point, café, exhibition and theatre space, office accommodation and activity rooms. Informal and lifelong learning opportunities will be provided for the local community through design workshops, local history classes and genealogy events. The building's architecture and artefacts, such as its memorial tablets and stained glass windows, which will be brought out of storage for reuse during the restoration process, will be interpreted and used to tell the story of the church and those who worshipped there. The histories of local figures whose contribution impacted upon the local and national stage will also be explored and featured.

Working with Consarc Conservation, a conservation management plan was prepared and a knowledge and understanding of the evolution of the church itself and the setting was invaluable in assisting in developing appropriate proposals. Before proceeding, a detailed survey of the building including a condition, structural and dimensional survey, were carried out. This included a digital 'Point Cloud', a detailed 3D survey of the whole of the building.

Prior to the decision to develop the site into a centre for arts, culture and heritage, Doherty Architects and the Trust had to consider how various uses would impact on the listed building. The spatial volume of the church had to be respected. Understanding the history of the building allowed consideration to be taken of the changing plan form and the need to preserve an understanding of the evolved facility as a part of its character.

Any insertions into the volume of the church will be made in a manner that is reversible. All new floors will be inserted on their own independent structure with significant shadow gaps where walls are met, ensuring the actual and visual dominance of the original structure. It has been deemed essential to successfully integrate smaller spaces, acoustic separation and fire escape facilities into the building without adversely affecting the character.

The architects used a 'building information model' to seek out opportunities to use the existing construction to satisfy new needs and the same model comprised of existing, demolition and new build data. This included utilising existing doors, louvres and vents. They used the ability to flip to 3D at any time to check where they could make necessary interventions that would not be visible from the main road, for example using the valleys between the main roofs. The 3D model was invaluable in determining appropriate routes for main services runs so that they can be integrated into the design, and it ensured that the visual impact of any interventions was fully understood while assisting in the retention of material which may otherwise have been altered. The development strategy allowed the design to utilise adjacent parts of the site to minimise the repetition of facilities. Designing a small link building allowed the three original parts of the complex to work as one building. Most importantly, the opening of a main entrance to the Antrim Road will ensure a public face to the new centre and give a new lease of life to this historic and significant Belfast church.[1]

| *Jill Kerry*

Note:
1. The author is grateful for information received from Doherty Architects; further information is available from the 174 Trust.

Background Information
www.174trust.org

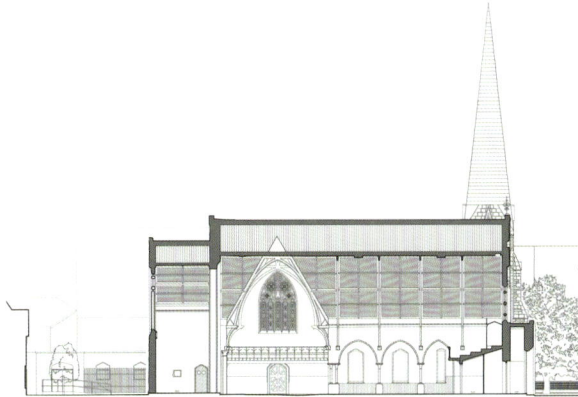

Existing Long Section

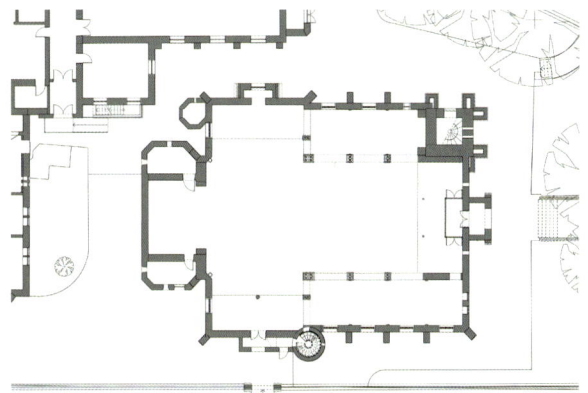

Existing Ground Floor Plan

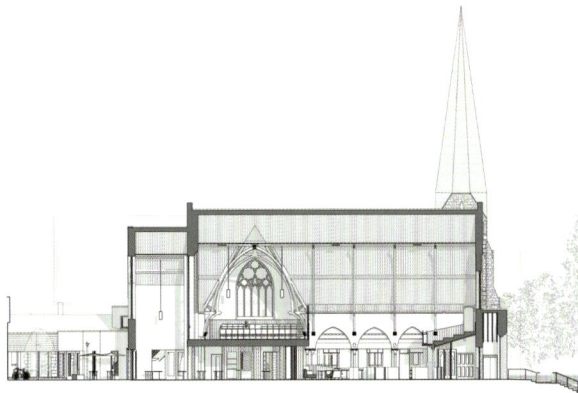

Proposed Long Section

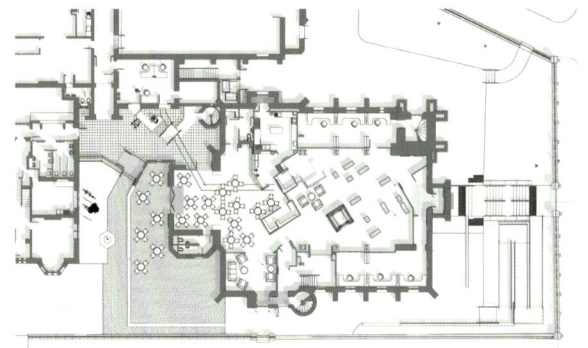

Proposed Ground Floor Plan

Rendered view

Rendered view

Carlisle Memorial Church, Belfast

The former Carlisle Memorial Methodist Church, Gothic masterpiece of W.H. Lynn, was built between 1875 and 1876. It closed as a place of worship in 1982, having been Belfast's Methodist 'cathedral' for over 100 years. With only limited use for the next decade or so, the building's condition deteriorated quickly. Thirty years after its closure a major programme of regeneration is now required to restore Carlisle Memorial as a vibrant and productive place.

Constructed of Comber sandstone and Armagh limestone, the church was built by local merchant James Carlisle to be a visible and significant memorial to his deceased children. Marking the gateway to North Belfast, Carlisle Memorial Church evokes a sense of the importance and prestige that Carlisle Circus once had as one of Belfast's most affluent areas.

Belfast Buildings Preservation Trust became involved with the Church in 1997. Founded in 1996, the Trust works to achieve both physical and social regeneration through the reuse of historic buildings. In 2008, the Trust became actively involved with the building through the launch of a community listening exercise. This produced a clear and decisive expression by the local communities that they recognise the value of the building, identifying it as a character marker for the area and highlighting the regeneration potential that it holds.

Based on its parlous condition, but conscious of the potential for its reuse to have a beneficial impact in the future, B.B.P.T. nominated Carlisle Memorial Church for inclusion on the World Monument Fund Watch. This biennial list of the world's most endangered historic and cultural sites has included globally recognised sites such as the Taj Mahal, the Great Wall of China and La Sagrada Familia. Carlisle Memorial's successful inclusion on the 2010 W.M.F. Watch ensured international recognition for the building.

Since then B.B.P.T. has acquired a 999-year lease on the building and, having done so, undertook a structural survey in 2011. The outcome of the survey confirmed the worst possible scenario, with the structural integrity of the roof in question and the identification of potentially dangerous loose stone. Securing the necessary funding, the Trust completed emergency stabilisation works in May 2012 to secure the roof, make the building weather-proof and remove loose stone and vegetation from the building's exterior.

The aim of this work, and of the Trust's efforts in the short term, is to secure a future for Carlisle Memorial Church. B.B.P.T. has identified that the process of regeneration will need to be phased, not least because of the costs involved but also to ensure that the outcome is a sustainable and economically beneficial reuse. The stabilisation works were the crucial first step in a decade-long effort. Without them there was a real risk that the building would be lost and, with it, the regeneration possibilities for North Belfast.

Church from Carlisle Circus

Detail of projecting transept

The seemingly intractable economic, physical and social issues that exist in North Belfast are of critical importance to how the process of regenerating Carlisle Memorial Church evolves. No one issue is of more importance than another. A successful reuse, with a purpose that looks to the future, requires that this context be considered alongside the historic nature of the building. A holistic, area based programme of work is necessary to help the communities identify the shape and form of regeneration in North Belfast. B.B.P.T. aims to evolve an ambitious project at Carlisle Memorial that is focused on how the building's reuse can best help the communities achieve tangible economic development, whilst capitalising on the character importance of the building for the place in which it is located.

In the report of its community listening exercise, B.B.P.T. concludes that 'The argument needs to be made that these solutions [to the various problems identified in North Belfast] can, and should, come from within the local community. Such an argument would have huge symbolic support from a regenerated Carlisle Memorial Church.'[1] The same report identifies that any project needs to be a collaborative one that helps to forge a common vision for regeneration and development in North Belfast. From both a strategic and practical perspective, this equates to an iterative process that evaluates both context and character, and the clear requirement to evolve a policy and practice of working with communities, government and business to evolve a regenerative project that seeks to address need and that is ambitious about what is achievable.

With stabilisation works complete, the Trust is now working on a second phase. This will encompass such permanent repairs as will allow the building to be brought back to limited use, focusing on re-roofing, re-flooring and re-glazing the building, with the addition of limited services. Of particular importance is the 'seeing-is-believing' factor, meaning that the outcome of phase 2, whilst not a fully restored building, must provide a productive and beneficial use. It is about being able to see change, protecting the building and using the time and space to work towards a long-term regeneration. Matching the various needs of the communities,

Top and bottom: condition of interior, 2012

the Trust's efforts are geared towards an interim use with a youth focus. This work is currently being costed in light of the recent stabilisation works but is estimated at between £1.5 and £1.9m.

Carlisle Memorial Church's potential to be a key piece of the regeneration jigsaw in North Belfast is premised on being ambitious about this potential and being ambitious about the common vision that local people, local businesses and government want to see realised in the area. B.B.P.T. has committed to developing a sustainable and appropriate reuse for Carlisle Memorial. This reuse must be developed by the range of stakeholders, with the local communities participating in the design, development and implementation stages as partners, not just as consultees. The heritage-led regeneration of Carlisle Memorial Church must underline ambition, must offer 21st-century potential, must underscore the Victorian authenticity of North Belfast and must declare the civic confidence of the North Belfast communities.

Belfast Buildings Preservation Trust, having worked on developing its own strategy for saving and reusing this internationally important building, will focus its regeneration efforts on economic development, enterprise, and creative entrepreneurship. It hopes that, in time, Carlisle Memorial Church will provide a space that the public, private and community sectors can use as a productive and beneficial centre for economic, physical and social regeneration. In short, Carlisle Memorial will one day be a place for creating ambitious, tangible and sustainable economic development in North Belfast.

| *Shane Quinn*

Note:
1. B.B.P.T, Restoration and reuse: Carlisle Memorial Church (Belfast, 2009), p. 29

Background Information
www.bbpt.org/carlisle.php

Chapel of the Resurrection, Belfast

Exterior side elevation and tower

In 1868, the third Marquis of Donegall started building the present Belfast Castle in North Belfast, under the lee of Cave Hill. Designed by Lanyon, Lynn & Lanyon, it was completed in 1870. During this period, the Marquis also built the mortuary chapel as a memorial to his son, Fredrick Richard, Earl of Belfast; also to designs by Lanyon, Lynn & Lanyon. Fredrick died and was buried in Naples, Italy in 1853. His body was initially exhumed and buried in the family vault in St Nicholas' Parish Church in Carrickfergus. When the new mortuary chapel was ready in December 1869, he was exhumed again and reburied in the vault beneath. The third Marquis brought the remains of a further six relatives to the vault. He himself was buried there in 1883. Brasses on the walls commemorated various members of both the Donegall and Shaftesbury families.

At the beginning of the First World War, services in the chapel were discontinued. However, it opened again in 1938, having been transferred with the freehold of the ground to the Church of Ireland by the Earl of Shaftesbury. Belfast Castle and its estate had been presented to the City Corporation four years earlier.

During the Second World War, the chapel suffered superficial damage during air raids but services continued every Sunday. In subsequent years, many Belfast parishes helped to keep the chapel going by conducting Sunday services there. The last service was held in 1972. The building had become impossible to maintain and the remains from the vault were cremated and returned to St Nicholas' Parish Church.

South Elevation

East Elevation

West Elevation

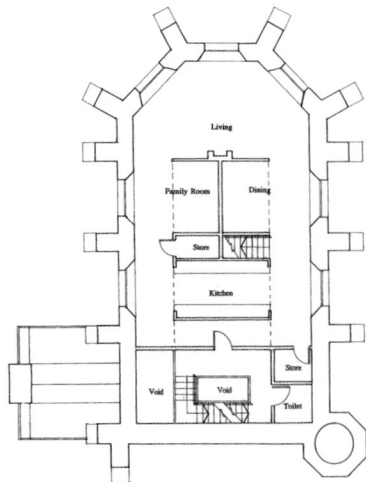

Ground Floor Plan

First Floor Plan

In 1982, the building was vandalised and the graves desecrated. Further vandalism and deterioration followed and eventually it was sold in 1985.

The site was privately acquired and a scheme was brought forward by a developer for a mixed housing scheme. Early negotiations with the Belfast Buildings Preservation Trust (B.B.P.T.) were undertaken, whereby the Trust would acquire the Chapel and some land surrounding it with a view to restoring and converting it. It was proposed that the Trust scheme would run in tandem with the developer carrying out the surrounding housing scheme. Due to the nature of the site: steeply sloping and entirely landlocked in behind suburban housing, the proposal was to bring in a new access road to the site directly off the Antrim Road.

The B.B.P.T. commissioned Hall Black Douglas Architects in 1997 to carry out a feasibility study on the possibility of converting the chapel to residential use. The study looked at the architectural implications of differing forms of subdivision and the financial viability of the preferred options. The agreed preferred option emerging was to convert the chapel to a single dwelling and Planning Permission and Listed Building Consent were duly sought and obtained in 2000.

The building is built in a decorated tall Gothic style. A circular side tower with conical slate roof sits on a tall four-bay nave with an apsidal end. It is built in a Scrabo sandstone with Portland limestone details. The roof has a very pleasant fish-scale detail in the slating.[1]

The design intention with such a conversion is to work with the original building in so far as it is possible - minimal intervention, reversibility in detailing and construction and the retention of the essence of the interior spatial character where possible. The Hall Black Douglas proposed scheme intends for the small-scale cellular bedrooms to be located on the ground floor with small windows inserted into the otherwise blank base level external walls – centred within the existing pier and buttress rhythm – the only external change proposed to the original building. The walls forming the cellular bedrooms then support the upper floor.

The main living areas are on an open plan first floor – the floor level set at the sill level of the main chapel windows. The rooms are arranged around a central core of kitchen, hearth and dividing partitions. This central core then supports a gallery above offering more study and living space – the gallery sitting in the centre of the full height volume and with views out of the tall original windows down over Belfast Lough and the wider city.

A vertical subdivision of space at the north gable end of the plan separates a fire-protected staircase offering secondary escape access from the balcony, and provides an entrance lobby at the front door porch. A separate staircase descends into the crypt.

Unfortunately the arrangement between the developers and the B.B.P.T. did not see the project through. The site changed hands with other housing schemes proposed, but, with recession biting, the site remains

External view of apsidal elevation

undeveloped today (2012). The chapel was reroofed in 2008 and the building made secure with good ventilation. It is hoped this will preserve its remaining structure and fabric until the economic climate makes the housing conversion attractive once more.

| *Stephen Douglas*

Note:
1. The building is Listed B+ and featured in the *Buildings at Risk, Vol.3*, p.21 (U.A.H.S.): BARNI ref. 26/51/001; HB ref: HB26/51/002. It features in Paul Larmour, *Belfast: an illustrated architectural guide* (Belfast, 1987), p. 37.

St Werburgh's, Dublin
A future as a place of worship and public venue

Interior showing the elaborate pulpit, gallery and organ case

St Werburgh's Church of Ireland church, originally built in the 12th century, remains one of the oldest active churches in Dublin. Situated inside the walls of Viking Dublin and at the heart of medieval Dublin, it is now part of the Christ Church Cathedral Group of Parishes. Much has been written about this magnificent building, its history – especially its involvement in the 1798 rebellion – and its association with the Chapel Royal in Dublin Castle. St Werburgh was the Abbess of Ely and daughter of Wulfhere and the church was first mentioned in a letter of Pope Alexander III dated 1179. The original church was destroyed by fire in 1301. Its replacement was in turn replaced in 1716 by a new church with a tall Baroque façade was designed by Thomas Burgh; however, it too was later largely destroyed by fire. The present church dates from 1759 and its fine interior has been widely admired. It is its connection with Dublin Castle – serving for a time as the Chapel Royal and where the Viceroy and his entourage worshipped – that has enabled St Werburgh's to survive the ravages of time, a dwindling congregation and the ever increasing cost of maintaining such an important church in the heart of Dublin.

Since the mid 1990s, St Werburgh's has undergone minor restoration works including re-roofing, re-pointing the front facade and the repair and conservation of the two large front doors. In 2004, the Select Vestry made a momentous decision to join forces with Dublin Castle, the O.P.W. (Office of Public Works) and Music Network to 'manage' the church building so that it could be used by all parties for concerts, lectures, exhibitions and to continue to provide church services. For such a

Staircase detail and wall memorials beneath gallery

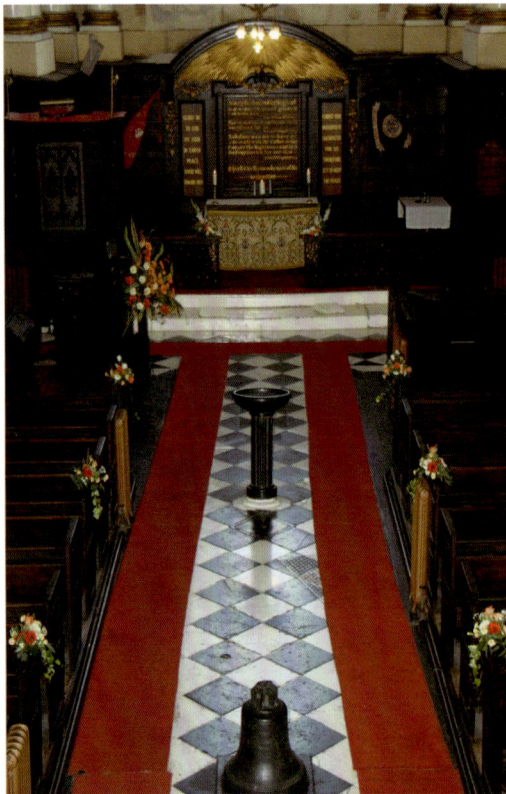

Central aisle looking towards communion table and reredos

project to work, all four groups were to finance the complete restoration and conservation of the church estimated to cost in the region of €1.8m and €2.2m. Unfortunately, two of the four groups pulled out of the arrangement so the restoration/conservation project fell back on the shoulders of the parish and its small number of parishioners.

Not to be deterred, the Select Vestry decided to proceed with the project on its own but over a phased basis. In 2010, sufficient funds were raised to begin and ultimately complete Phase One. For almost one year, the church remained closed for worship and re-opened in mid 2011. The works consisted of minor repairs to the roof, re-pointing the exterior of the entire church, conservation of the 18th-century windows and completely re-plastering the vaulted ceiling. The exterior re-pointing was undertaken to prevent water penetration. Given the thickness of the walls, the full extent of water penetration is unknown but was evident by severe dampness in certain areas of the church.

Many of the sash windows are amongst the earliest intact group of surviving sash windows in the city and these were repaired and overhauled. Given the extent of cracking to wall and ceiling plaster within the church and cracking to the external masonry, it was obvious that a considerable amount of movement had occurred in the structure of the church. To alleviate this problem, a series of steel channels and cables were introduced to provide restraint to the walls. These tie the north and south chancel walls together (at two levels over the

Detail of central doorway, front façade

ceilings) and tie the east wall back to the east wall on the south side of the nave. Thankfully, the roof timbers were in good condition with little or no evidence of historic decay or insect infestation. The work has been carried out by Hamilton Young & Associates Architects together with Paul Arnold Architects.

With Phase One complete, the Select Vestry plans to undertake the remaining restoration and conservation work over a period of between two and ten years (unless substantial funding is received). Phase Two will consist of a complete re-wiring of the church. Phase Three will see the restoration of the 'vestry room' and adjoining toilets together with the re-plastering of the west, north and south interior walls. Phase Four will consist of the conservation and restoration of the chancel and sanctuary areas together with the ornate stucco work over the sanctuary. Finally, Phase Five will see the conservation of the Victorian encaustic tiles in the porch area as well as the Portland stone and Kilkenny marble tiles in the centre aisle.

What does this all mean? With Phase One complete, the parish has once again joined forces with Dublin Castle in promoting this unique church building, primarily as a place of worship but also as a venue for concerts and exhibitions and now forms part of the Dublin Castle 'experience' with the church open to the public five days a week (apart from service times): from 2012 the church doors are open to the public from Tuesday to Saturday (10am-5pm). In addition, St Werburgh's stands right in the middle of a new walking tour which begins at Trinity College Dublin and finishes at St Catherine's Church in Thomas Street. The benefits of completing Phase One and opening the church on a regular basis is that more and more people pass through its doors to experience its beauty, learn about its history and take time out of their busy lives to simply sit and be quiet in what is commonly known as 'the jewel of Dublin's churches'.

| *David Pierpoint*

Contributors

| *Stephen Douglas* graduated from Q.U.B., winning the R.I.B.A. Dissertation Prize on 'The reuse of redundant churches'. In his subsequent 25 years in practice as a Director in the Belfast architectural firm Hall Black Douglas, he has kept an interest in the evolution of church buildings, their adaptation and reuse, as well as the design of new places of worship. He is currently working with the Belfast Buildings Preservation Trust to secure the future of Carlisle Memorial Church, cited in the World Monuments 2010 Watch List of the world's most endangered built heritage.

| *David Evans* spent his academic career from the early 1970s as a member of staff in the School of Architecture at Q.U.B. He co-authored a number of books including: *Introduction to Modern Ulster Architecture* (1977), *The Diamond as Big as a Square* (1981), *Queen's, an Architectural Legacy* (1995) and *Modern Ulster Architecture* (2006), all published by the U.A.H.S. In 2002 he provided 30 watercolours for the book *South Belfast: Terrace and Villa*. Having exhibited widely as an artist, he has been an Honorary Academician of the Royal Ulster Academy of which he was President from 1983 to 1993 and a Gold Medallist (1975). He has written extensively for *Perspective*, and has served on the committees of the U.A.H.S., Hearth and the Historic Buildings Council. He was conferred Honorary Membership of the R.S.U.A. in 2011.

| *Mary Hanna* is an architect and was architectural advisor with the Heritage Council from 1996 to 2004. Her responsibilities included the design of the Council's architectural grant system, the administration of architectural grants and the development of the Council's architectural heritage policy. She introduced the Conservation Plan methodology to Ireland in 1999, and co-ordinated the publication and implementation of conservation plans for many of Ireland's major historic sites. Since 2004 she has completed conservation plans for St Patrick's Cathedral, Dublin and the King's Inns in Dublin. She is a Trustee of the Irish Landmark Trust and in 2001 was elected to fellowship of the R.I.A.I.

| *Paul Harron* is a communications professional, a former architecture and built environment specialist at the Arts Council of N.I. and was senior architecture & design editor at Laurence King Publishing and editor at Phaidon Press. He holds a PhD from Q.U.B. on the work of Young & Mackenzie Architects of Belfast and degrees from the University of St Andrews and the University of London. A contributor to a wide range of publications including *Perspective*, he is a member of the Historic Buildings Council, a past lay judge for the R.I.B.A. Awards, a member of the boards of Hearth and Arts Care and sits on the committee of the U.A.H.S. He was conferred with Honorary Membership of the R.S.U.A. in 2007.

| *Frank Keohane* is a chartered building surveyor accredited in building conservation by the Royal Institute of Chartered Surveyors. Born in Cork, he is currently working on the *Buildings of Ireland* volume for his native city and county. Over the last decade he has overseen the conservation and repair of a wide variety of buildings with particular emphasis on ecclesiastical projects including Christ Church Cathedral and St Werburgh's church in Dublin as well as churches large and small across Ireland.

| *Jill Kerry* is one of the Trustees of the U.H.C.T. Following attendance at Bloomfield Collegiate School, she trained as an architect at Q.U.B., qualifying in 1986. She has been working exclusively in the conservation field for the past twenty years, in both the public and private sector. Although interested in all styles of architecture, she has a fascination for 20th-century architecture in Ireland and Great Britain, particularly Edwardian and post-war architecture.

| *William Laffan* was born in Dublin and studied at Oxford and London Universities. His books on Irish art include *The Cries of Dublin by Hugh Douglas Hamilton* (2003); *Misclenaea Structure Curiosa* (2005) and *Thomas Roberts, Landscape and Patronage in Eighteenth-Century Ireland* (2009, with Brendan Rooney). He has contributed essays to many exhibition catalogues including *A Time and a Place, Two Centuries of Irish Social Life* at the National Gallery of Ireland (2006); *A Question of Attribution, the Arcadian Landscapes of John Butts and Nathaniel Grogan* at the Crawford Art Gallery and *From Highwood To Home* at the Glucksman Gallery, Cork (both 2012). He is currently collaborating with Kevin Mulligan on a monograph on Russborough, Co. Wicklow, for the Alfred Beit Foundation.

| *Caroline Maguire* qualified as an architect in 1992. She has worked for N.I.E.A. as a senior conservation architect for the past ten years having gained experience in practice in Dublin, Belfast and Fermanagh. She was awarded the Alan Gailey Fellowship in vernacular architecture is 1995 and has been a committee member of the U.A.H.S. and the Building Limes Forum Ireland.

| *Stephen McBride* was ordained in 1987 and is currently Vicar of Antrim Parish. He has been Archdeacon of the diocese of Connor since 2002. He studied Architecture at Q.U.B. and Theology at T.C.D. His doctoral research at Q.U.B. was in 19th-century architectural trends in the Church of Ireland. This was primarily an examination of the influence of the Oxford and Evangelical Movements and the Cambridge Camden Society and Gothic revival on ecclesiastical design. Along with Dr Paul Larmour, he wrote 'Buildings and faith: church building from medieval to modern' in *The Laity and the Church of Ireland, 1000 – 2000* (Dublin, 2002).

| *Neil McClure* is Honorary Secretary of the friends of Portaferry Presbyterian Church and an enthusiast for both architecture and the performing arts. He is the choirmaster of f.P.P.C.'s community choir and a very poor organist. By day he is Professor of Obstetrics and Gynaecology at Q.U.B.

| *Edward McParland* is a fellow emeritus of T.C.D. where he has lectured in the Department of the History of Art since 1973. He published James Gandon, *Vitruvius Hibernicus* in 1985, and *Public architecture in Ireland, 1680-1760* in 2001. With Nicholas Robinson he founded the Irish Architectural Archive and he is on the board of The Irish Landmark Trust.

| *Michael O'Boyle* is a Grade 1 Conservation Architect and a director of Bluett & O'Donoghue Architects. He has completed conservation projects at the Cathedral of the Assumption, Thurles; St Mary's Church, Castlegregory; St Kevin's Church, Dublin; and St Mary's Cathedral, Kilkenny. Other projects include Kilkenny Courthouse, Fethard Tholsel, and Rothe House, Kilkenny. A graduate of U.C.D., he was awarded the Rachel McRory Award for his 2003 M.U.B.C. thesis on Catholic institutional buildings of the 19th century. He is a member of the Heritage Council's standing committee on architecture and is consultant conservation architect to North Tipperary County Council.

| *Peter Pearson* is an historian, conservationist and artist with a lifelong commitment to the protection and enhancement of Ireland's architectural heritage. He initiated the Drimnagh Castle Restoration Project and has worked with An Taisce and the Irish Georgian Society and is a founder member of the Dublin Civic Trust, a member of the Heritage Council and an honorary life member of the Dun Laoghaire Historical Society. He has written *Between the Mountains and the Sea, Dun Laoghaire-Rathdown County, The Heart of Dublin* and *Decorative Dublin*.

| *David Pierpoint* has been Church of Ireland Archdeacon of Dublin since 2004 and has been the Vicar of the Christ Church Cathedral Group of Parishes in the historic heart of Dublin – including St Werburgh's – since 1995. He is a Canon of Christ Church Cathedral, Dublin.

| *Shane Quinn* is Development Officer for Belfast Buildings Preservation Trust. Originally from Co. Armagh, he has substantial experience of helping to deliver physical and social regeneration through the medium of historic buildings. The Trust's portfolio of current projects includes the Floral Hall, St Malachy's School and Carlisle Memorial Church for which he leads on an ambitious community engagement programme. He holds degrees in Modern History & Politics and in Marketing & Entrepreneurship and has an interest in communications, social innovation, creative entrepreneurship and the strengthening of civic capacities.

| *Alistair Rowan* trained as an architect in Edinburgh and took a PhD in architectural history at Cambridge. He held an Italian research bursary at Padua University and worked in journalism for *Country Life* magazine. A lecturer in the Department of Fine Art at the University of Edinburgh, he was later the first Professor of Art History in U.C.D., Slade Professor of Fine Art at Oxford and Principal of the Edinburgh College of Art. In 2001 he set up the undergraduate courses in Art History at U.C.C. Founder and editor of the Yale *Buildings of Ireland* series, he is now retired and lives in Dublin.

| *Gráinne Shaffrey* is an architect and urban designer and a principal of Shaffrey Associates Architects. She has been involved in a number of church and other historic building adaptation projects. Gráinne enjoys the challenges of such projects where the convergence of new uses with considered and creative design can assist broader sustainability objectives. She is a member of the editorial board of *Architecture Ireland* and co-edited the 2011 'Conservation and Reuse' Issue which originally featured the Triskel Church conversion.

| *Patrick Shaffrey* is an architect and town planner with an interest in the conservation and regeneration of Irish towns and villages. He was a founding member and first President of the Irish Planning Institute and former President of An Taisce, the National Trust for Ireland. Together with Maura Shaffrey, he has published books on Irish architecture and urbanism.

| *Primrose Wilson, C.B.E.* has a longstanding interest in historic buildings. She was the Chairman of Historic Buildings Council (1994-2000) and during her term of office initiated European Heritage Open Days in NI. Primrose's involvement with conservation bodies across Ireland has included the Heritage Council, the U.A.H.S. and the Irish Georgian Foundation; in 2006 she became the founder Chairman of the Follies Trust. In 1997 she was awarded an O.B.E. for services to conservation and in 2007 a C.B.E. She is an Honorary Member of the R.S.U.A. With her husband, Edward, she has restored a listed mill complex in County Tyrone.

Abbreviations:

N.I.E.A.   Northern Ireland Environment Agency
Q.U.B.   Queen's University, Belfast
R.I.A.I.   Royal Institute of the Architects of Ireland
R.I.B.A.   Royal Institute of British Architects
R.S.U.A.   Royal Society of Ulster Architects
T.C.D.   Trinity College, Dublin
U.A.H.S.   Ulster Architectural Historical Society
U.C.C.   University College Cork
U.C.D.   University College Dublin

Bibliography

The following bibliography is designed to aid further reading germane to the subject of Irish ecclesiastical architecture and its history, conservation and reuse, especially in the context of the buildings examined in this volume; however, it is not intended to be exhaustive. The detailed bibliography contained in *Maintaining our churches: a short guide* published by the Ulster Historic Churches Trust (2004, 2009) may also be of interest.

Bailey, Mark E., *Border heritage: tracing the heritage of the City of Armagh and Monaghan County,* Armagh, 2008

Bradshaw, Brendan and Keogh, Daire (eds), *Christianity in Ireland: revisiting the story,* Blackrock, Dublin, 2002

Breakey, J.C., *Presbyterian church architecture in Ireland,* Belfast, 1966

Brett, C.E.B., *Buildings of Belfast, 1700-1914* (revised edn), Belfast, 1985

Brett, C.E.B., *Buildings of County Antrim,* Belfast, 1996

Brett, C.E.B., *Buildings of County Armagh,* Belfast, 1999

Brett, C.E.B., *Buildings of North County Down,* Belfast, 1999

Brett, C.E.B. et al, *Georgian Belfast 1750-1850, maps, buildings and trades,* Dublin & Belfast, 2004

Brooke, Peter, *Ulster Presbyterianism,* Dublin, 1987

Brooks, Chris and Saint, Andrew (eds), *The Victorian church: architecture and society,* Manchester, 1995

Carson, John T., *The 1859 Revival in Ulster: a brief summary,* Belfast, 1958, (reprinted 2009)

Casey, Christine, *The buildings of Ireland: Dublin,* New Haven and London, 2005

Champneys, Arthur, *Irish ecclesiastical architecture,* London, 1910

Cherry, Bridget (ed.), *Dissent and the Gothic Revival,* London, 2007

Cole, Emily (Ed.), *A concise history of architectural styles,* London, 2003

Connolly, Sean, *Religion and society in nineteenth-century Ireland,* Dundalk, 1985

Costello, Peter, *Dublin city churches,* Dublin, 1989

Craig, Maurice, *The architecture of Ireland: from earliest times to 1880,* London and Dublin, 1982

Crook, J.M., *Victorian architecture: a visual anthology,* London, 1971

Crookshank, Ann O., *Irish sculpture from 1600 to the present day,* Dublin, 1984

Cruickshank, Dan (ed.), *Sir Banister Fletcher's A history of architecture,* Oxford (20th edn), 1996

Curl, James Stevens, *Victorian architecture: its practical aspects,* Newton Abbot, 1973

Curl, James Stevens, *Victorian architecture,* Newton Abbot, 1990

Curl, James Stevens, *The Victorian celebration of death,* Thrupp, 2000

Curl, James Stevens, *Death and architecture,* Thrupp (3rd edn), 2002

Curl, James Stevens, *Victorian churches,* London, 1995

Curl, James Stevens, *Classical churches in Ulster,* Belfast, 1980

Curl, James Stevens, *Victorian architecture: diversity & invention,* Reading, 2007

Davey, J. Ernest, *1840-1940 Centenary: The story of a hundred years – an account of the Irish Presbyterian Church from the formation of the General Assembly to the present time,* Belfast, 1940

De Breffny, Brian and Mott, George, *The churches and abbeys of Ireland,* London, 1976

Dixon, Hugh, *An introduction to Ulster architecture,* Belfast, 1975

Dixon, Roger and Muthesius, Stefan, *Victorian architecture,* London, 1985

Elliott, Marianne, *The Catholics of Ulster: a history,* London, 2000

English Heritage, *New uses for former places of worship,* London, 2010

Evans, David and Patton, Marcus, *The Diamond as big as a Square: an introduction to the towns and buildings of Ulster,* Belfast, 1981

Evans, David, Larmour, Paul et al., *Modern Ulster architecture,* Belfast, 2006

Evans, David and Larmour, Paul, *Queen's: An architectural legacy,* Belfast, 1995

Ferran, Denise (et.al), *Highlanes Gallery, Irish art from Nathaniel Hone to Nano Reid: The Drogheda Municipal Art Collection in context,* Drogheda, 2006

Gaffikin, Patrick, *A geological guide to the building stones of Belfast,* Belfast, 1999

General Assembly of the Presbyterian Church in Ireland, *General Assembly: 150 years of mission and service 1840-1990,* Belfast, 1990

Gillespie, Raymond and Neely, WG (eds), *The laity and the Church of Ireland, 1000-2000: all sorts and conditions,* Dublin, 2002

Gillespie, Raymond and Royle, Stephen, *Belfast: c.1600-c.1900: the making of the modern city,* Dublin, 2007

Gillespie, Raymond, *Early Belfast: the origins and growth of an Ulster town to 1750,* Belfast, 2007

Gillespie, Raymond and Kennedy, Brian P., *Ireland art into history,* Dublin & Colorado, 1994

Graham, B.J. and Proudfoot, L.J. (eds), *An historical geography of Ireland,* London, 1993

Griffin, David J. and Lincoln, Simon, *Drawings from the Irish Architectural Archive,* Dublin, 1993

Grimes, Brendan, *Irish Carnegie Libraries,* Dublin, 1998

Hanna, Denis O'D, *The face of Ulster,* London, 1952

Harbison, Peter, Potterton, Homan and Sheehy, Jeanne, *Irish art and architecture: from prehistory to the present,* London, 1978

Hardy, P.D. (ed.), *Twenty-one views of Belfast and its neighbourhood* (reprinted with notes and an Introduction by C.E.B. Brett), Belfast, 2005

Hempton, David and Hill, Myrtle, *Evangelical Protestantism in Ulster society, 1740-1890,* London, 1992

Hewitt, John, *Art in Ulster 1557-1957,* Belfast, 1977

Holmes, Andrew R., *The shaping of Ulster Presbyterian belief and practice 1770-1840,* Oxford, 2006

Holmes, Janice, *Religious revivals in Britain and Ireland 1859-1905,* Dublin, 2000

Holmes, R.F.G., *Our Irish Presbyterian heritage,* Belfast, 1985

Holmes, R.F.G., *The Presbyterian Church in Ireland: a popular history,* Dublin, 2000

Holmes, R.F.G. and Knox, R. Buick (eds), *The General Assembly of the Presbyterian Church in Ireland 1840-1990,* Coleraine, 1990

Hutchinson, Sam, *Towers, spires and pinnacles: a history of the cathedrals and churches of the Church of Ireland,* Bray, 2003

Jones, Alan and Brett, David, *Toward an architecture: Ulster,* Belfast, 2007

Kerr, R.J., *The Parish and Church of St George, Dublin,* Dublin, 1962

Kirkpatrick, Laurence, *Presbyterians in Ireland: an illustrated history,* Belfast, 2006

Larmour, Paul, Belfast: *An illustrated architectural guide,* Belfast, 1987

Larmour, Paul, *The architectural heritage of Malone and Stranmillis,* Belfast, 1991

Lewis, Samuel, *Topographical Dictionary of Ireland,* London, 1837

Macaulay, Ambrose, *Down and Connor: a short history* (date unknown, c.1990)

McParland, *Public architecture in Ireland, 1680-1760,* New Haven and London, 2001

McKinstry, R., Oram, R., Weatherup, R. & Wilson, P., *The buildings of Armagh,* Belfast, 1992

National Inventory of Architectural Heritage, *An introduction to the architectural heritage of County Kilkenny,* Dublin, 2006

National Inventory of Architectural Heritage, *An introduction to the architectural heritage of County Clare,* Dublin, 2009

National Inventory of Architectural Heritage, *An introduction to the architectural heritage of County Roscommon,* Dublin, 2004

National Inventory of Architectural Heritage, *An introduction to the architectural heritage of County Limerick,* Dublin, 2011

National Inventory of Architectural Heritage, *An introduction to the architectural heritage of County Carlow,* Dublin, 2002

National Inventory of Architectural Heritage, *An introduction to the architectural heritage of East Cork,* Dublin, 2009

National Inventory of Architectural Heritage, *An introduction to the architectural heritage of North Cork,* Dublin, 2009

National Inventory of Architectural Heritage, *An introduction to the architectural heritage of West Cork,* Dublin, 2011

National Inventory of Architectural Heritage, *An introduction to the architectural heritage of South Dublin,* Dublin, 2002

National Inventory of Architectural Heritage, *An introduction to the architectural heritage of Fingal,* Dublin, 2002

National Inventory of Architectural Heritage, *An introduction to the architectural heritage of County Galway,* Dublin, 2011

National Inventory of Architectural Heritage, *An introduction to the architectural heritage of County Kerry,* Dublin, 2002

National Inventory of Architectural Heritage, *An introduction to the architectural heritage of County Kildare,* Dublin, 2002

National Inventory of Architectural Heritage, *An introduction to the architectural heritage of County Laois,* Dublin, 2002

National Inventory of Architectural Heritage, *An introduction to the architectural heritage of County Leitrim,* Dublin, 2004

National Inventory of Architectural Heritage, *An introduction to the architectural heritage of County Longford,* Dublin, 2010

National Inventory of Architectural Heritage, *An introduction to the architectural heritage of County Louth,* Dublin, 2008

National Inventory of Architectural Heritage, *An introduction to the architectural heritage of County Meath,* Dublin, 2002

National Inventory of Architectural Heritage, *An introduction to the architectural heritage of County Offaly,* Dublin, 2006

National Inventory of Architectural Heritage, *An introduction to the architectural heritage of County Sligo,* Dublin, 2007

National Inventory of Architectural Heritage, *An introduction to the architectural heritage of Tipperary North,* Dublin, 2006

National Inventory of Architectural Heritage, *An introduction to the architectural heritage of Tipperary South,* Dublin, 2007

National Inventory of Architectural Heritage, *An introduction to the architectural heritage of County Waterford,* Dublin, 2004, 2010

National Inventory of Architectural Heritage, *An introduction to the architectural heritage of County Westmeath,* Dublin, 2007

National Inventory of Architectural Heritage, *An introduction to the architectural heritage of County Wexford,* Dublin, 2010

National Inventory of Architectural Heritage, *An introduction to the architectural heritage of County Wicklow,* Dublin, 2004

National Inventory of Architectural Heritage, *An introduction to the architectural heritage of Limerick City,* Dublin, 2008

O'Donoghue, Brendan, *The Irish County Surveyors 1834-1944,* Dublin, 2007

O'Neill, M. and Lawlor, B., *Heritage trail St Mullin's, Co. Carlow,* 1996

Oram, Richard, *Expressions of faith: Ulster's church heritage,* Newtownards, 2001

Patton, Marcus, *Central Belfast: a historical gazetteer,* Belfast, 1993

Pierce, Richard, Coey, Alastair, and Oram, Richard, *Taken for granted: a celebration of 10 years of historic buildings conservation,* Belfast, 1984

Presbyterian Historical Society of Ireland, *A history of congregations in the Presbyterian Church in Ireland, 1610-1982,* Belfast, 1982

Port. M.H., *Six hundred new churches: a study of the Church Building Commission 1818-1856 and its buildings activities,* London, 1961

Powell, Kenneth and de la Hay, Celia, *Churches – a question of conversion,* London, 1987

Potterton, Homan, *Irish church monuments 1570-1880,* Belfast, 1975

Rowan, Alistair, *The buildings of Ireland: North West Ulster,* Harmondsworth, 1979

Rowan, Alistair and Casey, Christine, *The buildings of Ireland: North Leinster,* Harmondsworth, 1993

Scarlett, Duncan, *Churches of the Church of Ireland dedicated to St George,* Lisburn, 2010

Scarlett, Duncan, *Dedicated to St Anne,* Drogheda, 2007

Sheehy, Jeanne, *J.J. McCarthy and the Gothic Revival in Ireland,* Belfast, 1977

Taylor, Richard, *How to read a church,* London, 2004

Ulster Architectural Heritage Society (U.A.H.S.) Lists

Walker, Simon, *Historic Ulster churches,* Belfast, 2000

Williams, Jeremy, *A companion guide to architecture in Ireland 1837-1921,* Dublin, 1994

Wilson, Primrose, *Maintaining our churches: a short guide,* Belfast, 2004 & 2009

Yates, Nigel, *The religious condition of Ireland, 1770-1850,* Oxford, 2006

Yates, Nigel, *Buildings, faith and worship: the liturgical arrangement of Anglican churches, 1600-1900,* Oxford, 1991

Bibliography compiled by Paul Harron

Acknowledgements

The editor wishes to thank Primrose Wilson and Jill Kerry for their immense contribution to the development and creation of this publication, one which was very much a collaborative editorial effort. The editorial team, therefore, would like to express its gratitude to all the authors who have so generously provided essays and case studies: Alistair Rowan for his erudite Introduction which sets the subject matter in context; Michael O'Boyle for his instructive flow chart and practical guidelines; Caroline Maguire of the N.I.E.A. for outlining the role of the statutory body in Northern Ireland; David Evans; Edward McParland; the Ven. Stephen McBride; William Laffan; Peter Pearson; Grainne Shaffrey; Patrick Shaffrey; Frank Keohane; Neil McClure; Shane Quinn; Stephen Douglas and the Ven. David Pierpoint. In the initial stages of this project valuable advice and guidance was given by Mary Hanna, Michael O'Boyle and Marc Ritchie, Architectural Conservation Advisor at the Department of Arts, Heritage and the Gaeltacht, for which much thanks to each. Also gratitude is due to the R.I.A.I. and the R.S.U.A. for both facilitating receiving expressions of interest at the outset and permitting the revised and augmented reproduction of articles which first appeared in their journals, *Architecture Ireland* and *Perspective*, respectively.

The editorial team also wishes to thank Alison Gault of G2 design for her work in designing the book so handsomely and seeing it through the design, production and printing stages with patience, professionalism and good humour.

The architectural firms involved with the church conversions were very helpful in sourcing information to the authors of the various case studies and essays on work in progress – in particular: Nathan Armstrong of Nathan Armstrong Architects; Joanne Curran and Roisin Donnelly of Consarc Design Group; Cork City Council; Helen Devitt; Michael Doherty of Doherty Architects; Stephen Douglas of Hall Black Douglas; Joseph Doyle Architects; Fergus Flynn Rogers; Turlough McKevitt and McKevitt Architects; Mary O'Carroll from Carroll Associates, Roscommon; John O'Connell from John O'Connell Architects; James A. O'Connor and Associates; Paddy Shaffrey and Grainne Shaffrey from Shaffrey Associates Architects; and James Slattery Architect. Deirdre Conroy's assistance in providing earlier details on the Congregational chapel at Kilmainham is also acknowledged.

The following individuals were most helpful in providing information and assistance in various ways: Herma Boyle; David Byers; Charles Duggan; Suzanne Duke; Yvonne Glavey; Maeve Higgins; the Revd Robert Lockhart; Evelyn Mullally; Aoife Ruane, Director of the Highlanes Gallery, Drogheda; and

Chris Sherry of Ulster Journals. Bridie Lawlor provided valuable information on the history of St Mullin's and David Molloy and John Burns assisted with background information on buildings in Roscommon. Johnny Maloney in Ennistymon organised access to St Andrew's and provided information. The Knockainey Historical & Conservation Society, Eliza O'Grady and Tom Cassidy assisted by providing information on Knockainey Church.

Visits were paid to many libraries for the essay on converting churches to libraries and the editorial team would like to acknowledge the assistance given by all the librarians concerned. In particular: Anne Callanan of Loughrea Library, Hamrock Ivor of Claremorris, Eileen O'Connor from Gort library and John Lawlor, Oranmore, who sourced historic photographs and additional information. Charlie and Dora Clarke suggested several libraries and provided contacts; Katriona Byrne gave valuable advice and information.

Photographic credits are provided separately and thanks are extended to all those who provided and gave permission for the reproduction of their images and architectural drawings; however, in addition, the publisher wishes to thank the following people who were very helpful in sourcing and providing photographs: Jehan Ashmore; Willy Cumming, Senior Architect, National Inventory of Architectural Heritage; Ivan Ewart of Q.U.B.; Tony Roche from the Photographic Unit, National Monuments Service, Department of Arts, Heritage and the Gaeltacht; and the Irish Architectural Archive which provided historic photographs.

Finally, the publisher wishes to thank those who have provided generous sponsorship for the publication: the N.I.E.A.; the Heritage Council; Ulster Garden Villages Ltd and the Esme Mitchell Trust.

Picture credits

The publisher wishes to thank all those who have generously provided photographic and illustrative material for use in this book and granted permission to reproduce them, as follows:

Abbreviations: T top; B bottom; M middle; C centre; L left; R right; TL top left; TR top right; BL bottom left; BR bottom right; ML middle left; MR middle right.